Gallery
of
American
Quilts

1860-1989   BOOK 2

◆ **American Quilter's Society**

P. O. Box 3290 • Paducah, KY 42002-3290

Notice

The quilts in this book are no longer for sale. They were offered by members of the American Quilter's Society in 1988 and 1989. Approximately 70% of these quilts were sold. The unsold quilts were returned to the members.

The price of a one-year subscription (4 issues – Item #3201) of the *Quilts For Sale Catalog* is $16.00. Each catalog contains more than 130 full-color photographs of quilts for sale with description and price. A single copy of the catalog is $5.00 (ask for the latest issue). Also available from the American Quilter's Society is *Gallery of American Quilts 1848-1988*. This book contains 500 quilts which were offered by members of AQS in 1987 and early 1988 (Item #1938 – $19.95 plus $1.00 postage). Send check, money order or MasterCard/VISA number and your order to:

American Quilter's Society
P.O. Box 3290
Paducah, KY 42002-3290

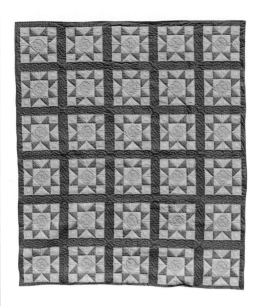

101688 - *TOP LEFT:* LOG CABIN BARN RAISING; 72" x 100"; primary colors/beige muslin prints; all cotton; made 1987 in Texas; machine pieced, hand quilted. Good quality pre-washed cottons, low-loft poly batt. Extra long for generous pillow tuck-under. Bright primary colors play against muslin & beige prints. Excellent condition. **$403.00**

201688 - *TOP RIGHT:* EVENING STAR; 70" x 84"; blues & dusty rose; 100% cotton fabrics; machine pieced, hand quilted. **$460.00**

301688 - *CENTER LEFT:* DAHLIA; 78" x 106"; pink & white; 100% cotton; made in 1988 in Pennsylvania; machine pieced, hand quilted; white background of poly & cotton. Cone border tiny soft rose bud print. **$391.00**

401688 - *CENTER:* BUTTERFLY; 67" x 82"; green, yellow with 56 multi-color butterflies; cotton; made in 1920s in Texas; hand pieced, quilted & appliqued; beautiful summer quilt; excellent condition with small age spots. **$288.00**

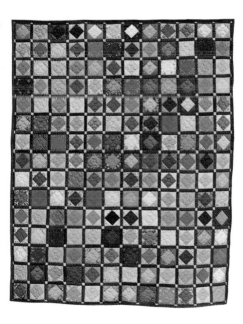

501688 - *CENTER RIGHT:* SQUARE IN SQUARE; 81" x 101"; multi-colors, soft beige backing; cotton, some blends; made in 1984 in California; hand pieced, hand quilted; all new fabrics, pre-shrunk, dye-set. No two blocks alike. **$403.00**

601688 - *BOTTOM LEFT:* PINWHEEL; 82" x 87"; cotton and cotton blends; made in 1980 in Kentucky; hand pieced, hand quilted; multi-colored prints on muslin background; centers of pinwheels solid colors; pillow included; light blue backing; polyester batting. **$460.00**

701688 - *BOTTOM RIGHT:* PIECED STAR; 77" x 77"; pink & white; cotton; made c. 1920 in Pennsylvania; machine pieced, hand quilted; maker's name on back; in very good condition. **$345.00**

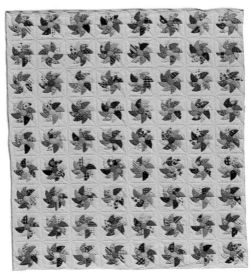

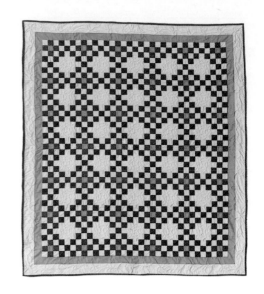

102688 - *TOP LEFT*: CHEYENNE; 58" x 58"; tones of blue, rust, black, tan and white; cotton & polyester; made in 1988 in Illinois; machine pieced, hand quilted; Center medallion is the Tea Basket design. **$299.00**

202688 - *TOP RIGHT*: WILD IRISH ROSE; 74" x 86"; ivory, green, rose & gold; cottons and cotton blends - prints & solids; made in 1983 in Minnesota; machine pieced, hand quilted; pattern was taken from *Quilter's Newsletter*. Good condition. **$322.00**

302688 - *CENTER LEFT*: COBBLE-STONES; 82" x 90"; made in 1987 in Kentucky; hand pieced, hand quilted; multi-colored prints on muslin background; polyester batting; light blue backing; pillow included; 575 "blocks." **$460.00**

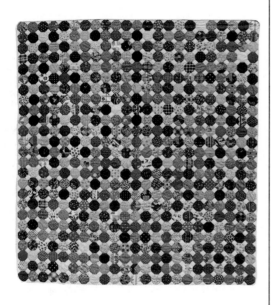

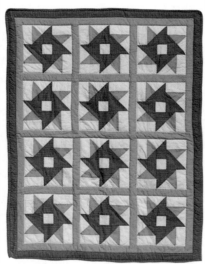

402688 - *CENTER*: WINDMILLS; 38½" x 48½"; light blue, colonial blue, white; cottons; made in 1986 in Connecticut; machine pieced, hand quilted; machine washable. **$115.00**

502688 - *CENTER RIGHT*: PHILADEL-PHIA PAVEMENT; 95" x 108"; blues with some dusty pink in prints with off-white background; 100% cotton, background poly & cotton; made in 1988 in Pennsylvania; machine pieced, hand quilted; Contains almost 3,000 pieces of 1½" blocks. **$598.00**

602688 - *BOTTOM LEFT*: TRI-SQUARE CHARM QUILT; 80" x 92"; multi-color, soft green backing; cotton, some blends; made in 1983 in California; hand pieced, hand quilted; all fabrics new, pre-shrunk, dye-set; no two blocks alike. **$403.00**

702688 - *BOTTOM RIGHT*: JOSEPH COAT; 72" x 87"; mixed colors; cotton & polyester blend; made in 1987 in Tennessee; hand pieced, hand quilted; good condition. **$253.00**

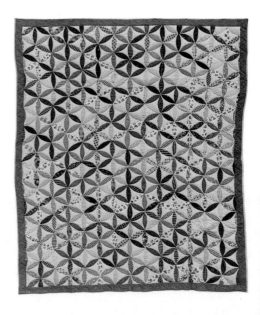

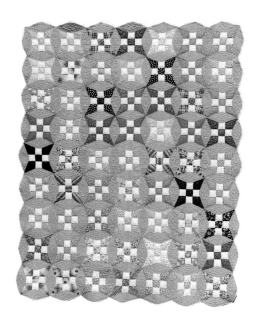

103688 - *TOP LEFT:* IMPROVED NINE PATCH; 78″ x 98″; assorted colors with apricot; cotton & polyester; made southern Illinois; hand quilted; an older top but quilted in 1987. $299.00

203688 - *TOP RIGHT:* STAR DAHLIA; 110″ x 113″; print with off-white; cotton; made in 1987 in Ohio; machine pieced, hand quilted; a nicely made quilt in an old fashion-looking print. Large enough for a king size bed; a thick batt of polyester was used to make it very puffy. $489.00

303688 - *CENTER LEFT:* MARTHA'S VINEYARD; 77″ x 93″; pink grapes, green vines on an off-white background; cotton & cotton polyester blends; made in 1987 in California; hand quilted; variety of Stearns and Foster pattern. $460.00

403688 - *CENTER:* NO NAME; 70″ x 80″; yellow, black; cotton; machine pieced, hand quilted; very colorful scrap quilt in an unusual pattern; quilter and date made are unknown. $150.00

503688 - *CENTER RIGHT:* SUNBONNET SISTERS; 68″ x 84″; multi-color; cotton; made c. 1930 in Pennsylvania; machine pieced, hand quilted; unique variation of a traditional pattern; very good condition. $432.00

603688 - *BOTTOM LEFT:* LULA'S TULIPS; 79″ x 80″; primary yellow, red, green, white background; red calico, white muslin, yellow cotton, red taffeta; made in 1987 in Michigan; machine pieced, hand quilted; bleach muslin bottom. $345.00

703688 - *BOTTOM RIGHT:* OHIO ROSE; 80″ x 80″; white background with pink & green; cotton/poly blend; made in 1981 in New York; hand quilted, hand appliqued; quilt won 1st place in applique in 1982 at New York State Fair; quilted with pink thread. $863.00

104688 - *TOP LEFT:* PLAID PARADISE; 70″ x 74″; jewel tones; cottons, silks, taffeta, woolens, calico, polyester, gabardine; made in 1987 in Michigan; machine pieced; tuffed, tied with crosheen; muslin bottom. **$156.00**

204688 - *TOP RIGHT:* SUNBONNET GIRL; 59″ x 94″; blue, white & multi-color; cotton & poly blend; made in 1988 in Michigan; machine pieced, hand appliqued, hand tied. **$202.00**

304688 - *CENTER LEFT:* DOTS OF FLOWERS; 75″ x 94″; saffron, soft green, red, white; cotton; made c.1890 in Pennsylvania; hand quilted, hand appliqued; very good condition. **$633.00**

404688 - *CENTER:* DOLLS OF THE NATIONS; 74″ x 86″; purple & white; cotton & poly blend; made in 1981 in Kentucky; machine quilted; hand painted; quilted in clam shell design; purple lining; polyester batting. **$230.00**

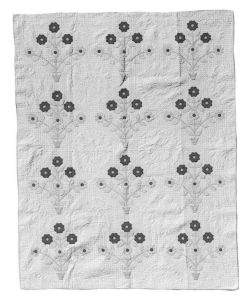

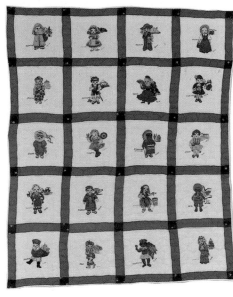

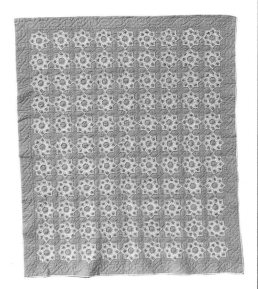

504688 - *CENTER RIGHT:* EVENING STAR; 87″ x 107″; teal with black; poly-mix, cotton; made in 1984 in Oregon; machine pieced, hand quilted; traditional batting; never used. **$230.00**

604688 - *BOTTOM LEFT:* CORN FLOWER; 79″ x 94″; pink; cotton blend; made in 1973 in California; hand pieced, hand quilted, border sewn on by machine; never used. **$575.00**

704688 - *BOTTOM RIGHT:* CELTIC CROSSROADS; 80″ x 96″; peach solid & floral print, brown, rust, green, gold and blue; cotton with muslin backing; made in 1987 in Pennsylvania; machine pieced, hand quilted; a cross motif fills the open blocks. **$575.00**

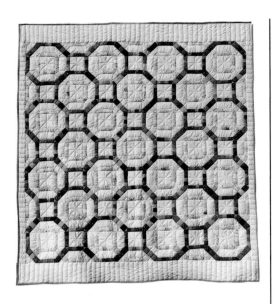

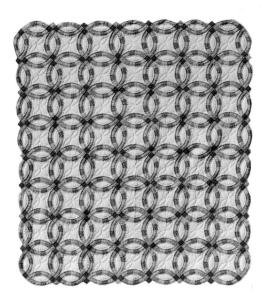

105688 - *TOP LEFT:* GARDEN WEDDING; 93″ x 103″; multi-colored white fill; polyester/cotton; made in 1987 in Missouri; machine pieced, hand quilted. **$345.00**

205688 - *TOP RIGHT:* DOUBLE WEDDING RING; 84″ x 94″; rust; cotton/poly blend; made in 1987 in Tennessee; machine pieced, hand quilted. **$374.00**

305688 - *CENTER LEFT:* LOG CABIN; 80″ x 104″; rust, tan; cotton/polyester; made in 1988 in Missouri; machine pieced, hand quilted; has extra plump bonded polyester fill. **$345.00**

405688 - *CENTER:* CARPENTER'S WHEEL; 72″ x 96″; pieced blocks, small floral prints in contrasting colors; 100% cotton; made in 1985 in Kentucky; hand pieced, hand quilted; blocks set together with unbleached muslin; feather circle design in solid blocks; quilted feather border. **$460.00**

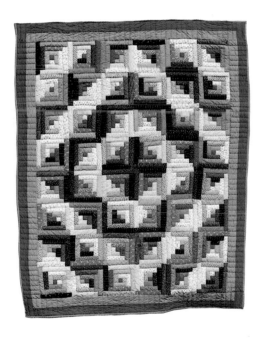

505688 - *CENTER RIGHT:* RAINBOWS; 80″ x 93″; orange, red, blue, green, yellow; cotton and cotton/polyester blend; made in 1987 in Minnesota; machine pieced, hand quilted; rainbows, ducks and hearts quilted throughout the quilt; all pre-washed fabrics; thick polyester batting. **$575.00**

605688 - *BOTTOM LEFT:* GOLDEN WEDDING RING; 106″ x 109″; multi-color; polyester & cotton; hand cut, hand pieced, hand quilted; **$403.00**

705688 - *BOTTOM RIGHT:* LOG CABIN STAR; 88½″ x 100″; blues; 100% prewashed cotton; made in 1986 in Ohio; machine pieced, hand quilted; quilt was washed after quilting to remove markings. **$547.00**

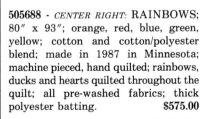

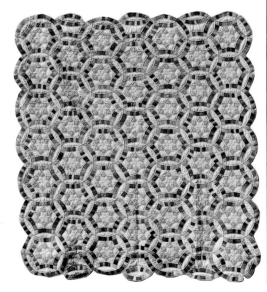

106688 - *TOP LEFT:* SISTER'S CHOICE; 72″ x 85″; dark blue & white; cotton and poly/cotton; made in 1982-84 in Oklahoma; machine pieced, hand quilted; double-size quilt; signed and dated; good condition.   **$397.00**

206688 - *TOP RIGHT:* DRESDEN FLOWER; 92″ x 103″; light purple & orchid print; cotton/polyester, bonded polyester batting; made in 1988 in Missouri; machine pieced, hand pieced, hand quilted.   **$345.00**

306688 - *CENTER LEFT:* FANCY FAN; 86″ x 106″; off-white, solid brown with rust, brown, beige & gold prints; cotton/poly blend; made in 1986 in Tennessee; machine pieced, hand quilted.   **$460.00**

406688 - *CENTER:* LOVERS KNOT; 55″ x 55″; pink, rose, greens; top quality 100% cotton, prewashed, won't shrink or bleed; made in 1987 in Colorado; machine pieced, hand quilted. **$184.00**

506688 - *CENTER RIGHT:* COUNTRY COLONIAL; 84″ x 96″; white background, embroidered gold, green, blue; cotton/poly blend; made in 1985-87 in New York; hand quilted; quilt won 1st place in Kit Category at New York State Fair in 1987; quilted with blue thread.   **$460.00**

606688 - *BOTTOM LEFT:* FALLING TIMBERS; 85″ x 96″; yellow, muslin; cotton; made in 1985 in Arkansas; hand pieced, hand quilted.   **$230.00**

706688 - *BOTTOM RIGHT:* OCEAN WAVES; 50″ x 50″; dark & light blue-green; cotton and poly/cotton; made in 1981 in Oklahoma; machine pieced, hand quilted; lap quilt, signed and dated; good condition.   **$253.00**

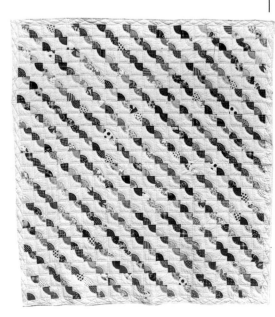

107688 - *TOP LEFT:* BEAR'S PAW; 82″ x 97″; dusty blue, berry, cream; top quality 100% cotton, prewashed, won't shrink or bleed; made in 1986 in Colorado; machine pieced, hand quilted; surrounded by a sawtooth border. $575.00

207688 - *TOP RIGHT:* BUTTERFLIES; 98″ x 102″; blues and rose; polyester & cotton; made in Kentucky; hand quilted, cross stitched and some embroidery. $460.00

307688 - *CENTER LEFT:* VARIATION OF CAT'S CRADLE; 93″ x 112″; predominantly brown with various accents; backing - 100% cotton; stuffing - polyester; top - mostly cotton; some cotton/poly blends; made in 1987 in Ohio; machine pieced, hand quilted. $575.00

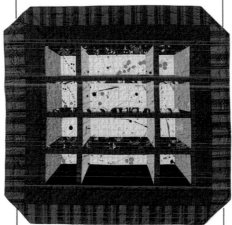

407688 - *CENTER:* ARTIST IN RESIDENCE; 42″ x 42″; burgundy & turquoise; cottons & blends; made in 1986 in Missouri; machine and hand pieced, hand quilted; contemporary adaptation of traditional "attic windows" pattern; award winner. $403.00

507688 - *CENTER RIGHT:* BOW TIE; 79″ x 94″; multi-color, beige background; cotton top, unbleached muslin back; made in 1920-30 in Missouri; hand pieced, hand quilted in 1986 with Dacron batting; good condition. $207.00

607688 - *BOTTOM LEFT:* TEACHER'S PET SAMPLER; 74″ x 102″; coordinated navy, cranberry, cream prints & solids, cranberry microdot back; 100% prewashed cottons; made in 1987 in Virginia; machine pieced, hand quilted; made by quilting teacher. $460.00

707688 - *BOTTOM RIGHT:* UNNAMED ORIGINAL DESIGN; 74″ x 90″; black, white, gray with green & red; backing - 100% cotton, stuffing - polyester, top - cotton & cotton/poly blends; made in 1986 in Ohio; machine pieced, hand quilted; wall hanging. $690.00

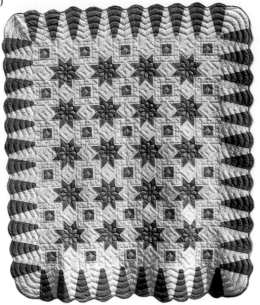

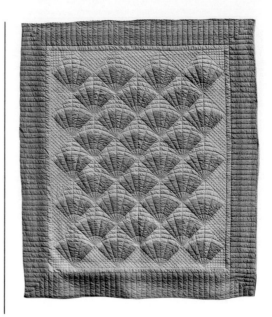

108688 - *TOP LEFT:* DAHLIA; 96″ x 110″; dusty blue, peach; cotton & cotton/poly; made in 1988 in Missouri; machine pieced, hand quilted; made by Mennonites in Missouri; Dacron batting; signed & dated. **$414.00**

208688 - *TOP RIGHT:* PEACHES AND CREAM; 89″ x 104″; peaches, apricots, creams; 100% cotton; made in 1987 in Virginia; machine pieced, hand quilted; fabrics prewashed; solid cream back; double fabric binding; bonded polyester batting; signed and dated. **$575.00**

308688 - *CENTER LEFT:* SAMPLER; 80″ x 113″; antique red & cream; 100% cotton; made in 1987 in the Philippines; machine pieced, hand quilted; sampler with ruffle border. **$345.00**

408688 - *CENTER:* TULIP; 32″ x 32″; pink, melon & tan; cotton & polyester; made in 1986 in Illinois; machine pieced, hand quilted. **$110.00**

508688 - *CENTER RIGHT:* COUNTRY ROSE; 85″ x 106″; burgundy and dusty rose; 100% cotton; made in 1987-88 in Pennsylvania; machine pieced, hand quilted; soft warm colors; all fabrics prewashed; clean and new. **$575.00**

608688 - *BOTTOM LEFT:* ROYAL STAR OF OKLAHOMA; 90″ x 95″; royal blue solid & print with light blue solid & print; polyester & cotton; made in 1988 in Missouri; machine pieced, hand quilted; white fill & light blue print lining; extra plump polyester batting. **$345.00**

708688 - *BOTTOM RIGHT:* ROYAL STAR OF GEORGIA; 90″ x 94″; dark rose, pink, burgandy; polyester & cotton; made in 1988 in Missouri; machine pieced, hand quilted; one of a series of Royal Stars of the States; white fill with white lining; extra plump polyester batting. **$345.00**

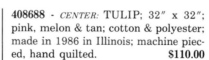

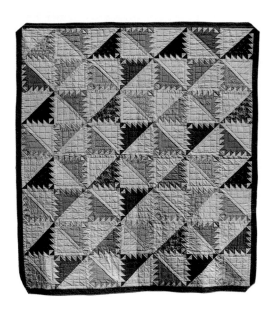

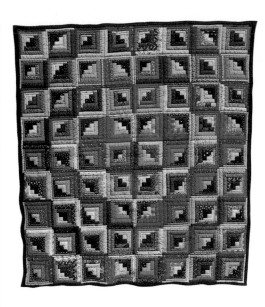

109688 - *TOP LEFT:* SAWTOOTH; 91″ x 102″; pink-rose to tan-browns with unbleached muslin; cotton/poly mix; made in 1988 in Oregon; machine pieced, hand quilted; made with comfortable soothing colors in a pleasing pattern with a cross hatching quilted pattern. **$259.00**

209688 - *TOP RIGHT:* MY SCRAPBAG HEART; 83″ x 94″; blues, reds, pinks; cotton & cotton blends; made in 1987 in Utah; machine pieced, hand quilted; 200 different prewashed fabrics used; made from off-centered log cabin blocks. **$403.00**

309688 - *CENTER LEFT:* TRIP AROUND THE WORLD; 90″ x 100″; browns; all new cotton, polyester batting, muslin lining; made in 1987 in South Carolina; machine pieced, hand quilted; materials prewashed; completely washable; binding is bias printed fabric; unbleached muslin lining; never used. **$460.00**

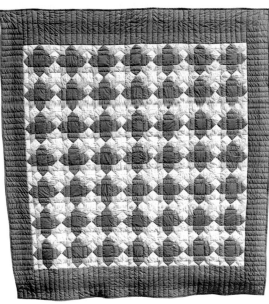

409688 - *CENTER:* WEATHER VANE; 94″ x 103″; blue; cotton/polyester; made in 1987 in Missouri; machine pieced, hand quilted; polyester batting. **$345.00**

509688 - *CENTER RIGHT:* LOG CABIN; 75″ x 104″; browns, rust lining; cotton, polyester batting; made in 1985 in South Carolina; machine pieced, hand quilted; all new materials; prewashed; completely washable; never used. **$345.00**

609688 - *BOTTOM LEFT:* LONE STAR; 45″ x 45″; navy blue prints; cotton & polyester cotton; made in 1988 in Missouri; machine pieced, hand quilted. **$115.00**

709688 - *BOTTOM RIGHT:* GOLDEN WEDDING RING; 90″ x 102″; multicolor prints & solids on white; broadcloth & cotton & polyester solids & prints; made in Illinois; machine pieced, hand quilted; unusual pattern with over 4,000 pieces; corner triangles & binding are red. **$460.00**

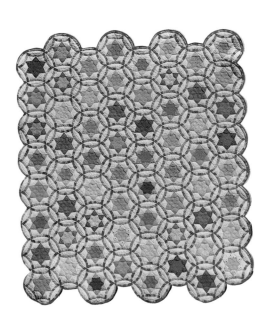

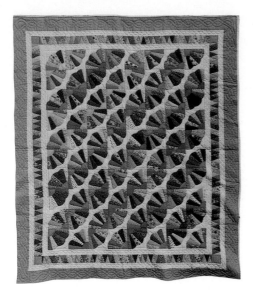

110688 - *TOP LEFT:* FAN; 85" x 103"; aqua border combined with ivory; muslin & bright cotton prints; made in 1985 in Illinois; machine pieced, hand quilted; fans are set together to suggest movement; bordered with triangles of bright prints; never used. **$403.00**

210688 - *TOP RIGHT:* FLOWER GARDEN BASKET; 100" x 108"; beige, brown; cotton, polyester; made in 1979 in Tennessee; machine pieced, hand quilted. **$345.00**

310688 - *CENTER LEFT:* WEDDING RING; 90" x 109"; beige, blue; cotton, polyester; made in Illinois; machine pieced, hand quilted; new quilt. **$259.00**

410688 - *CENTER:* OUT OF SILENCE; 35" x 52½"; black, blues, reds; cottons & blends; made in 1986 in California; machine pieced, hand quilted; original

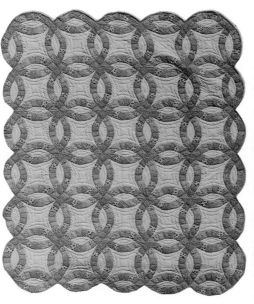

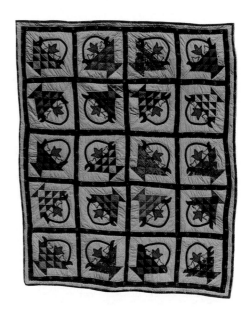

design from a traditional pattern; strips were machine sewn to the black squares instead of piecing two triangles. **$317.00**

510688 - *CENTER RIGHT:* BASKET OF FLOWERS; 72" x 88"; muslin background with black lining & yellow flowers; made in 1975 in Tennessee; machine pieced, hand quilted; hand appliqued. **$115.00**

610688 - *BOTTOM LEFT:* WHITE-ON-WHITE; 97" x 124"; unbleached muslin/beige; cotton, polyester; made in Illinois in 1988; hand quilted; reversible. **$230.00**

710688 - *BOTTOM RIGHT:* GIANT DAHLIA; 94" x 119"; pastels with blue border & back; cotton & cotton blends; made in 1986 in Wisconsin; machine pieced, hand quilted, hand appliqued; a blend of old & new prints to give a pastel look with a great deal of quilting. **$345.00**

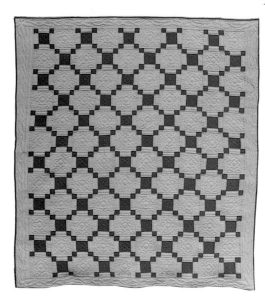

111688 - *TOP LEFT:* HEX ON BLOCKS; 72″ x 88″; print top, blue lining; cotton, polyester; made in 1980 in Tennessee; machine pieced, hand quilted. **$98.00**

211688 - *TOP RIGHT:* IRISH CHAIN; 92″ x 105″; light & dark blue; cotton, polyester; made in 1985 in Illinois; machine pieced, hand quilted. **$230.00**

311688 - *CENTER LEFT:* BOW TIE; 78″ x 86″; variegated colors, solid and print; cotton, polyester & cotton; made in 1981 in Arkansas; hand pieced, hand quilted; polyester batting; extra quilting. **$155.00**

411688 - *CENTER:* LONE STAR; 45″ x 45″; dusty blue & dusty rose mix; cotton, polyester & cotton; made in 1988 in Missouri; machine pieced, hand quilted. **$115.00**

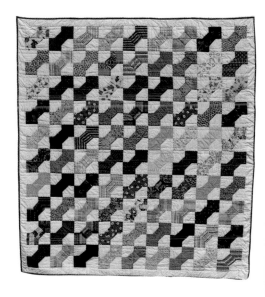

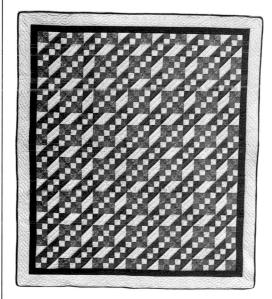

511688 - *CENTER RIGHT:* JACOB'S LAD-DER; 80″ x 91″; neutral browns and salmon; cotton and cotton/poly blends, backing is 100% cotton, batt is polyester; made in 1987 in California; machine pieced, hand quilted; contains 1,276 pieces. **$460.00**

611688 - *BOTTOM LEFT:* DOUBLE WED-DING RING; 91″ x 102″; royal blue, blue calicos, some beige; cotton/polyester blend; made in 1984 in Alabama; machine pieced, hand quilted; heart quilting between rings; queen size; ecru ruffle. **$458.00**

711688 - *BOTTOM RIGHT:* LOG CABIN; 89″ x 96″; brown, rust, red, white; 50% cotton/50% polyester; made in 1986 in Tennessee and Alabama; machine piec-ed, hand quilted; many small pieces make up this new quilt. **$432.00**

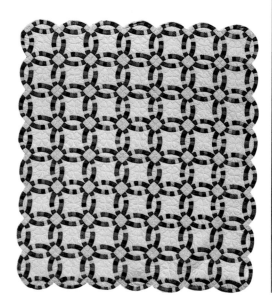

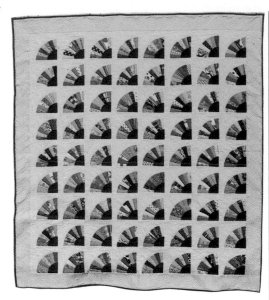

112688 - *TOP LEFT:* FAN; 96″ x 105″; multi-color prints with ivory border & back with chocolate brown accent; cotton & cotton blends; made in 1987 in Wisconsin; machine pieced, hand quilted, hand appliqued; fan pieced with over 245 different prints. **$345.00**

212688 - *TOP RIGHT:* LOG CABIN; 96″ x 120″; pink, brown, beige; cotton, polyester; made in 1988 in Illinois; machine pieced, hand quilted; large queen/king size. **$213.00**

312688 - *CENTER LEFT:* DRESDEN PLATE; 90″ x 107″; pink, white; cotton, polyester; made in 1986 in Illinois; machine pieced, hand quilted; 30 block Dresden Plate pattern. **$259.00**

412688 - *CENTER:* DIAMOND LOG CABIN; 73″ x 90″; purples, pinks; cotton & cotton blends; made in 1988 in Utah; machine pieced, hand quilted; all new prewashed fabrics. **$230.00**

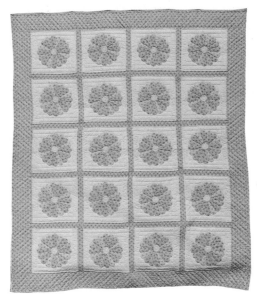

512688 - *CENTER RIGHT:* LOG CABIN; 91″ x 107″; rose, pink, blue, grey; cotton/polyester blend; made in 1986 in Illinois; machine pieced, hand quilted; large size. **$230.00**

612688 - *BOTTOM LEFT:* BROKEN STAR; 70½″ x 72″; mixed colors in prints & solids, pink star; cotton; made in 1945 in Kentucky; hand quilted, hand appliqued. **$374.00**

712688 - *BOTTOM RIGHT:* DAHLIA; 82″ x 94″; wine, rose, navy, white; cotton; made in 1987 in Illinois; hand pieced, hand quilted; 1935 pattern. **$317.00**

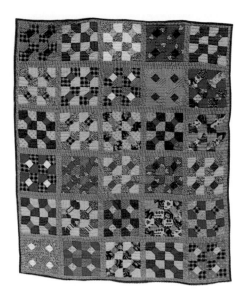

113688 - *TOP LEFT:* BOW TIE; 74″ x 87″; mixture of colors, grey lining; cotton; made in 1943 in Alabama; hand pieced, hand quilted; cotton batting. $288.00

213688 - *TOP RIGHT:* FLOWER GARDEN; 85″ x 102″; variety of colors, yellow centers with green and off-white; cotton; made in 1987 in Illinois; machine pieced, hand quilted. $253.00

313688 - *CENTER LEFT:* SISTER'S CHOICE; 79″ x 96″; blue print with rose & cream; polyester & cotton; made in 1987 in Arkansas; machine pieced, hand quilted; blue with ½″ squares with tiny flowers in each square; rose & cream to finish out the top; poly batting; poly & cotton lining; quilted around each seam. $230.00

413688 - *CENTER:* FLOWER GARDEN; 72″ x 87″; red, green & assorted prints; cotton; made in 1955 in Kentucky; hand pieced, hand quilted; scalloped with red as the primary color; lightweight. $230.00

513688 - *CENTER RIGHT:* TUMBLIN' STAR; 96″ x 100″; blue, rust; cotton; made in 1981 in Alabama; machine pieced, hand quilted; poly batting. $345.00

613688 - *BOTTOM LEFT:* OTTO THE GIRAFFE; 44″ x 54″; yellow, brown; cotton; made in 1979 in California; hand pieced, hand quilted; copyrighted pattern. $110.00

713688 - *BOTTOM RIGHT:* TRIP AROUND THE WORLD; 68″ x 76½″; multi-color; cotton; made in 1955 in Kentucky; hand pieced, hand quilted; blocks are about 1¼″ each of multi-color prints and solids; good condition, but two sections frayed about 2″ on hem. $173.00

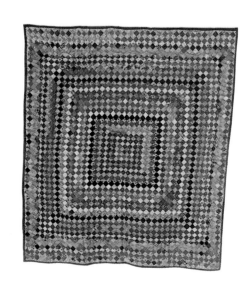

114688 - *TOP LEFT:* STATE BIRD AND FLOWER; 70″ x 87″; light blue, white, multi-color; cotton; made in 1955 in Kentucky; hand pieced, hand quilted; birds & flowers are embroidered; lightweight. **$575.00**

214688 - *TOP RIGHT:* STAR AND CRESCENT; 87″ x 103″; red, yellow, white; cotton/polyester blend; made in 1987 in Missouri; machine pieced, hand pieced, hand quilted; poly batting. **$460.00**

314688 - *CENTER LEFT:* CARTWHEEL; 60″ x 80″; yellow background, printed "wheels"; cotton; made in 1938 in New England; hand pieced, hand quilted; mutli-colored printed cottons form the spokes of wheels on yellow background; wide flowered border; border scalloped on two sides; good condition. **$345.00**

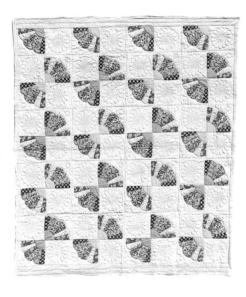

414688 - *CENTER:* TRIP AROUND THE WORLD; 80″ x 94″; variety of colors; soft polyester knits; made in 1986 in Kentucky; hand pieced, machine quilted; durable. **$230.00**

514688 - *BOTTOM RIGHT:* FANS & MEDALLION; 73″ x 85″; yellow, white, multi-color; cotton; made in 1920s in Texas; hand pieced, hand quilted; can be reversible; material excellent; few age stains barely noticable. **$288.00**

614688 - *BOTTOM LEFT:* SCRAPS; 77″ x 92″; multi-colored scraps; cottons, cotton/polyester blends; made in 1988 in North Carolina; machine pieced, tied; old fashioned look achieved with variety of prewashed prints, some solids, blue cotton backing; unused. **$230.00**

714688 - DEVIL'S PUZZLE; 78″ x 94″; peach solid, various prints; cotton/polyester blend; made in 1987 in Missouri; both machine & hand pieced, hand quilted; polyester batting. **$460.00**

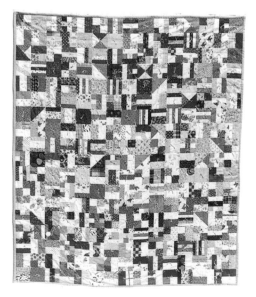

115688 - *TOP LEFT:* IRISH CHAIN VARIATION; 72″ x 90″; muslin, solid rust, dark blue print with rust; cottons & cotton/polyester blend; made in 1985 in North Carolina; machine pieced, hand quilted; flower & leaf design quilted in muslin area; straight lines on rust & print; muslin back; unused. $483.00

215688 - *TOP RIGHT:* FLORAL CAMEO; 80″ x 96″; gold & yellow on white; all cotton, polyester low-loft batt; made in 1986 in Idaho; hand quilted, hand appliqued; top stitched around the inner edge of each petal & leaf; single stitch method; reversible. $690.00

315688 - *CENTER LEFT:* SAMPLER; 84″ x 117″; cream, mauve, burgandy; cotton/polyester blend; made in 1988 in the Philippines; machine pieced, hand quilted. $345.00

415688 - *CENTER:* CRAZY ANIMALS #5; 23″ x 36½″; mixed colors; cottons; made in 1987 in Maine; machine pieced, hand quilted; pieced crazy quilt to be used as wall hanging; all new fabrics. $138.00

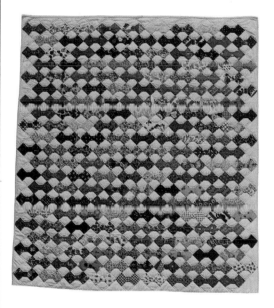

515688 - *CENTER RIGHT:* BABY BOW TIE; 43″ x 49″; yellow background with bow ties of various prints; cotton & cotton blends; made in 1988 in Kentucky; hand pieced, hand quilted; small pillow included. $87.00

615688 - *BOTTOM LEFT:* ON TOP OF THE DAWN; 51″ x 51″; blue, lavendar, grey; cotton, blends; made in 1986 in California; machine pieced, hand quilted; inspired by the early dawn in Banff, Canada; colors were selected to float, contrasted by the dark blue; excellent condition. $460.00

715688 - *BOTTOM RIGHT:* AMISH SHADOWS; 28½″ x 28½″; shades of blue & pinks against black; 100% cotton solids, polyester batt, cotton muslin backing; made in 1987 in California; machine pieced, hand quilted; wallhanging contains over 250 squares, each slightly over 1″; borders are all mitered at corners; should be hung diagonally. $144.00

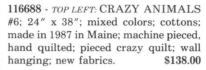

116688 - *TOP LEFT:* CRAZY ANIMALS #6; 24″ x 38″; mixed colors; cottons; made in 1987 in Maine; machine pieced, hand quilted; pieced crazy quilt; wall hanging; new fabrics. $138.00

216688 - *TOP RIGHT:* LONE STAR; 41″ x 41″; peach prints; cotton, polyester & cotton; made in 1988 in Missouri; machine pieced, hand quilted. $115.00

316688 - *CENTER LEFT:* STAR BRIGHT; 38½″ x 52″; rose, teal, green accents; cottons & blends; made in 1986 in Missouri; hand pieced, hand quilted; whole & segmented hexagons in non-traditional interpretation; award winner. $403.00

416688 - *CENTER:* IRISH CHAIN; 50″ x 50″; dark Williamsburg blue, blue print; 100% cotton, polyester batting; made in 1987 in Indiana; machine pieced, hand quilted; embroidered center flowers in country blue. $144.00

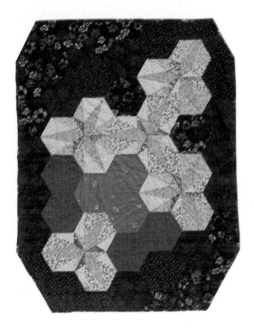

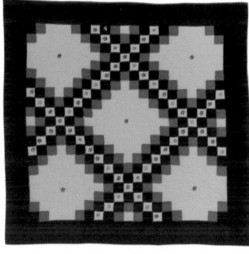

516688 - *CENTER RIGHT:* EMBROIDERY CRIB QUILT; 38½″ x 51″; polyester/-cotton blend; made in 1987 in Tennessee; hand embroidered, hand quilted. $69.00

616688 - *BOTTOM LEFT:* RUBIC'S CUBE STAR; 55″ x 55″; black with 5 shades of green, red & blue; cotton; machine pieced, hand quilted; wallhanging or tablecloth was made when rubic's cube was popular; original pattern. $230.00

716688 - *BOTTOM RIGHT:* IRISH CHAIN WITH FINISHED CHAIN; 36″ x 36″; black with red & blue chain; cotton; made in 1987 in Pennsylvania; machine pieced, hand quilted; wallhanging made with Amish colors; thick batt; quilted with shamrock design. $144.00

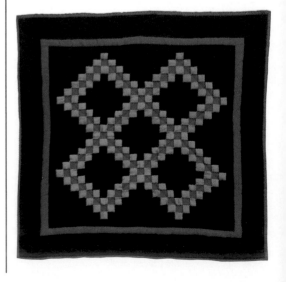

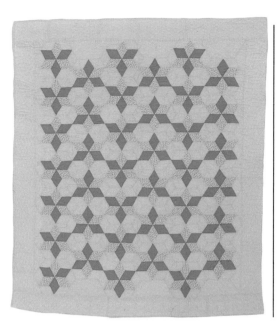

117688 - *TOP LEFT:* TUMBLING BLOCK; 74″ x 86″; yellow, gold; cotton & polyester; made in 1987 in Indiana; hand pieced, machine quilted. $144.00

217688 - *TOP RIGHT:* BROKEN STAR; 89″ x 89″; rainbow colors; cotton & polyester; made in 1987 in Indiana; machine quilted; hand pieced; over 1,100 diamonds in pattern; backing white cotton & polyester; polyester batting. $167.00

317688 - *CENTER LEFT:* YO-YO; 62″ x 91″; variegated colors; 100% cotton; made in 1927 in Illinois; hand pieced; true Yo-Yo quilt with no batting; never used. $144.00

417688 - *CENTER:* ROMAN STRIPE; 50″ x 50″; black, multi-colored; 100% cotton; made in 1987 in Indiana; machine pieced, hand quilted; traditional quilt done in Amish style. $144.00

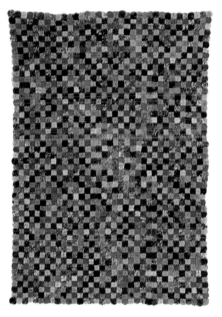

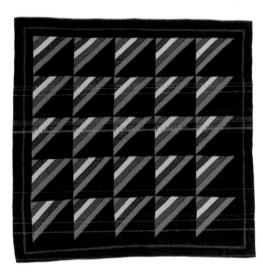

517688 - *CENTER RIGHT:* BETHLEHEM STAR - BLAZING STAR; 74″ x 96″; grey, blue, gold, purple; mostly 100% cotton, a few 50/50 pieces, cotton batting and back; made in 1986 in Arkansas; machine pieced, hand quilted; replica of an 1880 quilt; has been washed to assure no dye bleed; geometric purple back; never used. $207.00

617688 - *BOTTOM LEFT:* ALL WHITE QUILT; 108½″ x 110½″; muslin, all white; cotton; made in 1985 in Pennsylvania; hand quilted; pineapple circle quilted in center of quilt; corner of quilt is turned back in order to fit entire quilt in picture. $805.00

717688 - *BOTTOM RIGHT:* GIANT ZINNIA; 78″ x 96″; mauve, periwinkle on white; 100% cottons; made in 1986 in Hawaii; machine pieced, hand quilted; four corners are quilted with heart & feather pattern; bonded polyester batting; backing solid white. $575.00

118688 - *TOP LEFT:* OHIO ROSE; 72″ x 77″; white, green, rose; cotton/polyester blend; made in 1987 in Kentucky; machine pieced, machine quilted, machine appliqued; very durable; white lining; polyester batting. **$161.00**

218688 - *TOP RIGHT:* GRAND-MOTHER'S FLOWER GARDEN; 80″ x 82″; variegated colors; cotton; made in 1950s in Kentucky; hand pieced, hand quilted; polyester batting; used, but in good condition. **$144.00**

318688 - *CENTER LEFT:* INSPIRATION BLOCK; 52½″ x 70¼″; ivory, tan, dark brick red; cotton; made in 1988 in Connecticut; machine pieced, hand quilted; lots of quilting on each block. **$230.00**

418688 - *CENTER:* EVENING SHADOWS; 29″ x 39″; teal green, tan, aqua; cottons; made in 1986 in Minnesota; machine pieced, hand quilted. **$81.00**

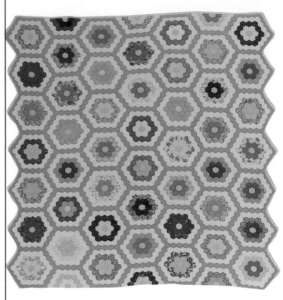

518688 - *CENTER RIGHT:* STRIPE RAIL; 51″ x 73″; red, white & blue; 100% cotton; made in 1987 in Hawaii; machine pieced, hand quilted; batting is bonded polyester. **$259.00**

618688 - *BOTTOM LEFT:* TRIP AROUND THE WORLD; 83½″ x 68½″; cotton; made in 1950 in Tennessee; hand pieced, hand quilted; very colorful with blendings of varied colors making up the design, has slight fading on border. **$288.00**

718688 - *BOTTOM RIGHT:* LOG CABIN; 86″ x 110″; blue; cotton/polyester; made in 1987 in Missouri; hand quilted, machine pieced; large quilt with plump polyester fill. **$345.00**

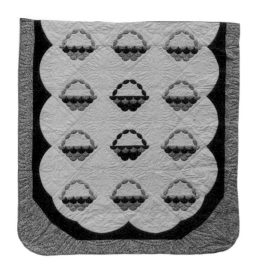

101988 - *TOP LEFT:* CLAMSHELL BASKET; 83″ x 89″; Pink, rose, wine; 100% cotton face, poly batting, 65% poly & 35% cotton blend back; made in 1985 in Wisconsin; hand quilted & appliqued; hand appliqued clamshells. Pillow shams included. 1987 first prize winner.$1,725.00

201988 - *TOP RIGHT:* "THE CROSS"; 83″ x 88″; brown cross with shaded cream to gold colors around it, border of purple & navy with forest green for hill; pre-washed poly-cotton blends; made in 1985 in Texas; machine pieced, hand quilted; John 3:16 embroidered on quilt. $403.00

301988 - *CENTER LEFT:* DRESDEN PLATE; 85″ x 106″; multi-color plates w/yellow centers, brown borders, muslin background; 100% cottons, all prints except muslin; made in 1988 in Virginia; machine pieced, hand quilted & appliqued; poly batt, double bound edges. $547.00

401988 - *CENTER:* PINWHEELS; 46″ x 71″; olive, tangerine & black; 100% cot-

ton; made in 1987 in Hawaii; machine pieced, hand quilted; bonded poly-batting; cable quilted border. Doubled bias binding; tangerine quilting thread. $265.00

501988 - *CENTER RIGHT:* "THE TWELVE DAYS OF CHRISTMAS"; 90″ x 108″; multi-colored (predominantly red & green); muslin, cottons, polycotton blends; made in 1982 in Connecticut; machine pieced, hand quilted & appliqued; depicts 12 days of Christmas. $1,265.00

601988 - *BOTTOM LEFT:* EVENING SHADOWS; 81″ x 100″; green; cottons & cotton blends; made in 1988 in Utah; machine pieced, hand quilted; this quilt contains 18 different pre-washed green fabrics arranged from light to dark. There are 3,431 rectangles, each 1″ x 2″. $460.00

701988 - *BOTTOM RIGHT:* PINWHEEL; 69½″ x 85″; black/all colors of plain solid broadcloth; all cotton/polyester blend broadcloth; made in 1988 in Minnesota; machine pieced, hand quilted; back of quilt is black broadcloth. $460.00

102988 - *TOP LEFT:* MONKEY WRENCH; 81″ x 90″; print with sold green, border is green; cotton & polyester; made in 1984 in Arkansas; machine pieced, hand quilted; quilted around each seam with straight lines in border; white backing. **$190.00**

202988 - *TOP RIGHT:* TRIP AROUND THE WORLD; 84″ x 104″; light wine to burgundy; all cotton; made in 1988 in Texas; machine pieced, hand quilted. **$345.00**

302988 - *CENTER LEFT:* CHURN DASH; 83″ x 102″; light gray, dark gray & dark red; all cotton; made in 1988 in Kentucky; machine pieced, hand quilted; made with Jenny Beyer fabrics; feather wreath quilting in plain blocks. **$345.00**

402988 - *CENTER:* "A DIFFERENT LOG CABIN"; 47″ x 61″; light & dark multi-colored calicos with midnight blue print back & binding; cotton & cotton-polyester; made in 1987 in Colorado;

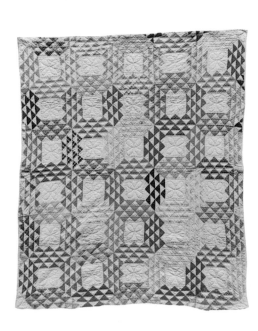

machine pieced, hand quilted, machine quilted; unusual log cabin arrangement. **$202.00**

502988 - *CENTER RIGHT:* DAHLIA; 96″ x 110″; dusty blue & mauves; cotton/poly; made in 1988 in Missouri; machine pieced, hand quilted; medium-dark dusty blue background & mauve print & petals, off-white background & back. Dacron batting. Signed & dated. **$403.00**

602988 - *BOTTOM LEFT:* OCEAN WAVES; 57″ x 71″; various calicos, ginghams & plaids on white; cotton; made in 1870-1880 in Indiana; hand pieced, hand quilted; small four leaf clover shape quilted in the white squares. **$345.00**

702988 - *BOTTOM RIGHT:* 4 POINT STAR; 78″ x 96″; variegated prints & white; cotton/poly; made in 1988 in Missouri; machine pieced, hand quilted. **$317.00**

103988 - *TOP LEFT:* LONE STAR; 92″ x 94″; mainly blues, some gold & wine, cream background & backing; cottons, cotton/poly blends; made in 1950's in North Carolina; machine pieced, hand quilted; piecing not 100% perfect, but fine stitches & double quilting more than off-set it. Done on very thin batting. Bound in blue on cream background. Never used. $460.00

203988 - *TOP RIGHT:* GRANDMOTHER'S FAN-TASY; 70″ x 71″; multi-colored; lace appliques, satins, upholstery fabrics, velvets, brocades, taffeta; made in 1982 in Connecticut; hand pieced, hand appliqued; Moire fans arranged so that the edges touch to form a central medallion with serpentine borders. Embroidered seams & touches with lace & ribbon appliques. $805.00

303988 - *CENTER LEFT:* AUTUMN MAPLE LEAVES; 75″ x 88″; red, yellow, brown, tan, green & white; cotton; made c. 1935 in Pennsylvania; hand

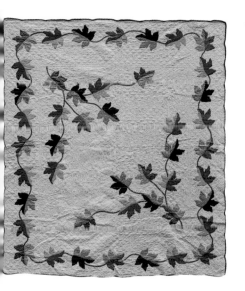

quilted, hand appliqued; co-ordinated pillowcases are included. $489.00

403988 - *CENTER:* JOSEPH'S COAT OF MANY COLORS; 72″ x 84″; polyester cotton blends; made 1980 in Kentucky; 100% polyester fiberfill; hand quilted; made from 2½″ squares. $288.00

503988 - *CENTER RIGHT:* HEARTS ABOUND; 42″ x 54″; dusty pinks/dusty blues; 100% cotton; made in 1987 in Colorado; hand quilted, hand appliqued; each heart is stuffed. $202.00

603988 - *BOTTOM LEFT:* DRUNKARD'S PATH; 83½″ x 65″; blue & yellow; made in 1986 in Tennessee; hand pieced, hand quilted. $345.00

703988 - *BOTTOM RIGHT:* ROSE; 86″ x 100″; cotton, poly/cotton blends; made in 1987 in Alabama; hand pieced, hand quilted, hand appliqued; each block color coordinated; hand appliqued, polyester batting. $322.00

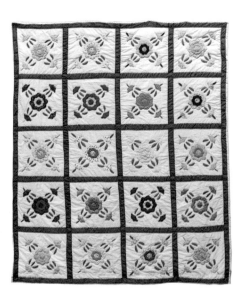

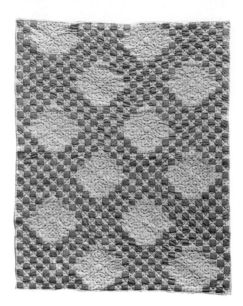

104988 - *TOP LEFT:* TRIPLE IRISH CHAIN; 76" x 96"; robin egg blue; cotton & cotton/poly; made in 1988 in Missouri; hand pieced, hand quilted; white & blue print, blue solid, Dacron batting. **$196.00**

204988 - *TOP RIGHT:* WEATHERVANE; 76" x 91"; variegated prints & solid with white cotton; cotton & some blends, backing is muslin; made in 1987 in Arkansas; hand pieced, hand quilted; each block is print & solid with filling of off-white, quilted around each seam. **$230.00**

304988 - *CENTER LEFT:* LOG CABIN; 82" x 101"; light blue to navy blue; all cotton; made in 1988 in Kentucky; machine pieced, hand quilted. **$345.00**

404988 - *CENTER:* SUNFLOWER; 84" x 94"; marigold, emerald, chocolate & white; cotton; made c. 1940 in Pennsylvania; hand pieced, machine pieced, hand quilted. **$460.00**

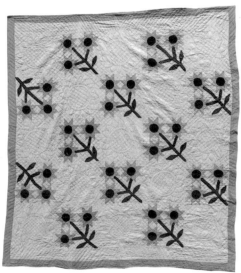

504988 - *CENTER RIGHT:* ROSE OF SHARON; 73" x 85"; multi-color with light orange background; silk/polyester blend with inlaid print; made in 1988 in Michigan; machine pieced, machine quilted. **$173.00**

604988 - *BOTTOM LEFT:* VIRGINIA REEL; 75" x 95"; blue/burgundy; cotton; made in 1986 in Tennessee; has a white background with burgundy & blue being the primary colors. **$259.00**

704988 - *BOTTOM RIGHT:* LOG CABIN; 97" x 103"; wine & lavender with block border; cotton; made in 1987 in Alabama; machine pieced, hand quilted; red with gold print lining, poly batting. **$368.00**

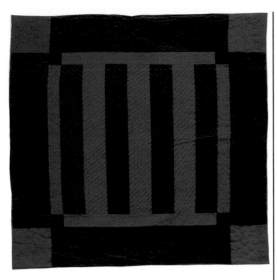

105988 - *TOP LEFT:* AMISH BARS; 96″ x 96″; red & blue; cotton & polyester; made in 1987 in Wisconsin; machine pieced, hand quilted. **$345.00**

205988 - *TOP RIGHT:* ORIENTAL PUZ-ZLE; 85″ x 85″; blue; cottons & cotton blends; made in 1987 in Utah; machine pieced, hand quilted; quilt contains 32 different pre-washed fabrics. Design was inspired by a rug seen in a Japanese magazine. Fluffy comforter size. $345.00

305988 - *CENTER LEFT:* CHERRY BASKETS; 88″ x 103″; white, navy/med. blue print, white/med. blue print; 100% cotton; made in 1987 in Ohio; machine pieced, hand quilted, hand appliqued; beautifully hand quilted with pansies in baskets, feathers, hearts, leaves, lattice. **$495.00**

405988 - *CENTER:* IMPROVED NINE-PATCH; 76″ x 90″; pastel 9-patches with pink star in middle; cotton; made in

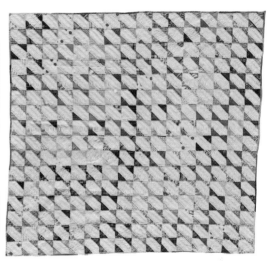

1940's in Michigan; machine pieced, hand quilted; pink star enhances the pastel 9-patches which surround it; quilted in 2″ grids. **$156.00**

505988 - *CENTER RIGHT:* INDIAN HAT-CHET; 85″ x 85″; assorted scraps of all colors; cotton & polyester blends; made in 1984 in Arkansas; machine pieced, hand quilted. **$230.00**

605988 - *BOTTOM LEFT:* BOW TIE; 72″ x 82″; variegated prints; cotton & cotton/poly blends; made in 1986 in Kentucky; hand pieced, hand quilted; quilt made of durable fabrics, polyester padding, cotton fleece lining. **$173.00**

705988 - *BOTTOM RIGHT:* BICENTEN-NIAL; 88″ x 90″; red, white & blue; cotton/polyester blend; made in 1976 in Idaho; machine pieced, hand quilted, hand appliqued; pattern created to celebrate Bicentennial with 13 stars that point to 1976; won blue ribbon at county fair. **$432.00**

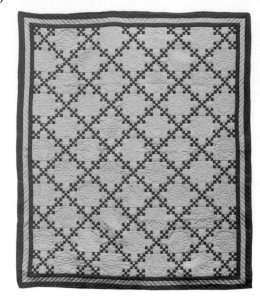

106988 - *TOP LEFT:* DOUBLE NINE PATCH; 85″ x 102″; red & white; all cotton; made in 1988 in Kentucky; machine pieced, hand quilted; quilted with feather wreath. **$345.00**

206988 - *TOP RIGHT:* LONE STAR; 92″ x 107″; red; cotton/poly; made in 1986 in Missouri; machine pieced, hand quilted; white background & back, red print, Dacron batting. **$374.00**

306988 - *CENTER LEFT:* SOLOMON'S PUZZLE; 67″ x 84″; rose, indigo, tan; cotton; made c. 1900 in Pennsylvania; hand pieced, hand quilted. **$443.00**

406988 - *CENTER:* SWEET DREAMS; 70″ x 80″; polyester/cotton blend fabric, 100% polyester fiberfill, polyester/cotton printed lining; made in 1987 in Kentucky; machine pieced baby sleeping in the flower garden, dreaming about sleeping on the moon with stars shining bright. **$230.00**

506988 - *CENTER RIGHT:* BASKET; 82″ x 92″; mulberry/cream; 100% cotton; made in 1987 in Colorado; machine pieced, hand quilted; charming baskets & bows are enhanced by many hearts in the quilting designs, done in contrasting off-white quilting thread. A Best of Show in 1987. **$575.00**

606988 - *BOTTOM LEFT:* LONE STAR; 69″ x 76½″; multi-color; cotton; made c. 1940 in Kentucky; hand pieced, hand quilted; quilted in diamonds, very old-fashioned looking. **$345.00**

706988 - *BOTTOM RIGHT:* GRANDMA'S FAN; 88″ x 103″; multi-colored; cotton-polyester blend; made in 1988 in Idaho; hand & machine pieced, hand quilted; hand appliqued; colors to match old style quilts used in grandmother's time, Wild Rose pattern quilted in each block. **$345.00**

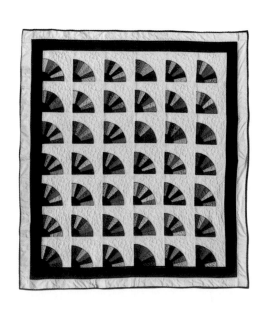

107988 - *TOP LEFT:* GARDEN OF TULIPS AND BUTTERFLY; 81″ x 103″; rice, roses, mauve, Chinese blue, black & wine; 100% cotton; made in 1988 in Ohio; hand quilted, hand appliqued; beautifully hand quilted feathers, flowers, vines & heart shaped leaves. **$495.00**

207988 - *TOP RIGHT:* FANS; 94″ x 106″; shades of blue; cotton; made in 1987 in Pennsylvania; machine pieced, hand quilted; beautiful color combination of blues has ¼″ stitching around each fan & heart swags quilted in the border. **$489.00**

307988 - *CENTER LEFT:* DRESDEN PLATE; 79″ x 92″; assorted colors with yellow centers; cotton & polyester blends; made in 1987 in Arkansas; machine pieced, hand quilted; polyester batting. **$259.00**

407988 - *CENTER:* FIELD OF DIAMONDS; 72″ x 94″; red, green & yellow; 50-50 cotton & poly blends; made in Kentucky; machine pieced, machine

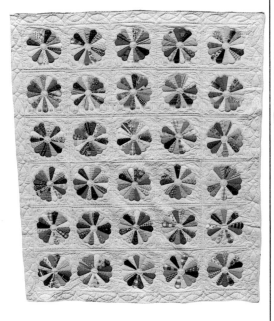

quilted; muslin lining, Mountain Mist batting. **$173.00**

507988 - *CENTER RIGHT:* DOUBLE WEDDING RING; 80″ x 90″; orange/yellow/green on white background; cotton; made in 1985 in Virginia; hand pieced, hand tied. **$115.00**

607988 - *BOTTOM LEFT:* MARINER'S COMPASS; 91″ x 91″; blue, gray & white; 100% cottons with polyester batting; made in 1986 in Indiana; machine pieced, hand quilted, hand appliqued; has won 2 People's Choice Awards & 2 blue ribbons, sea monsters quilted in ocean area, gray backing. **$690.00**

707988 - *BOTTOM RIGHT:* RED CROSS STITCHED ROSE; 82″ x 86″; red cross stitched rose with green cross stitched leaves; cotton; made in Missouri; machine pieced, machine quilted; backing is white cotton. **$202.00**

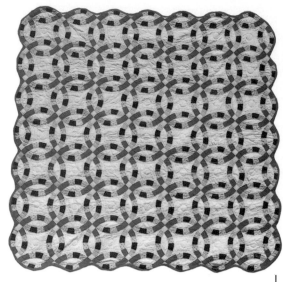

108988 - *TOP LEFT:* DOUBLE WEDDING RING; 86½″ x 94″; cotton/cotton blends; made in 1988 in Tennessee; machine pieced, hand quilted; multi-color with red/gold predominating, beige background, binding is red. There is a second one, 82″ x 82″, with yellow instead of gold (not pictured). $345.00

208988 - *TOP RIGHT:* ART DECO FLOWERS; 91″ x 91″; navy, purple, black & pink; poly/cottons; made in 1987 in Indiana; machine pieced, hand quilted, hand appliqued; blue ribbon winner, flowers in an Art Deco style, lots of quilting, sleeve for hanging, appliqued vines and buds, navy backing. $690.00

308988 - *CENTER LEFT:* DAHLIA; 96″ x 108″; dusty rose, cotton & cotton & polyester; made in 1988 in Missouri; machine pieced, hand quilted. $391.00

408988 - *CENTER:* GRANDMOTHER'S FLOWER GARDEN; 78″ x 86″; flowers in various prints & plains with yellow

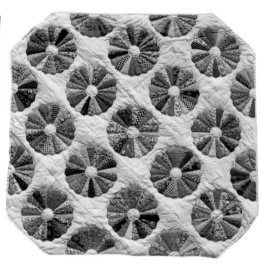

centers & white outline, light blue backing & binding; cottons & cotton blends; made in 1987 in Montana; machine pieced, hand quilted; every hexagon is quilted inside with fine quilting stitches, loads of quilting, straight edges. $374.00

508988 - *CENTER RIGHT:* DRESDEN PLATE; 65″ x 65″; multi-colored white background; cotton & polyester; made in 1988 in Michigan; machine pieced, hand quilted; all washable fabrics, polyester batting, pre-washed. $345.00

608988 - *BOTTOM LEFT:* CHRISTMAS STAR; 54″ x 54″; red, green & white; 100% cottons, polyester filling; made in 1988 in California; machine pieced, hand quilted; decorative Christmas quilt, can be used as a tablecloth, wallhanging, sofa throw or bed topper. $230.00

708988 - *BOTTOM RIGHT:* LONE STAR; 77″ x 86″; brown, orange, yellow & white; cotton; made in Missouri; machine pieced, hand quilted; white cotton backing. $282.00

109988 - *TOP LEFT:* LONE STAR QUILT; 104″ x 104″; peach, cotton & polyester/cotton; made in 1988 in Missouri; machine pieced, hand quilted. **$391.00**

209988 - *TOP RIGHT:* SALT, SUGAR AND FEED SACKS; 60″ x 80″; orange; cotton; made in 1885 in New Mexico; machine pieced, hand quilted; fair condition. **$259.00**

309988 - *CENTER LEFT:* GOOD MORNING GLORY; 80″ x 96″; blue & rose; cotton/polyester; made in 1988 in Missouri; machine pieced, hand quilted; navy, medium blue & dark blue prints with a contrast of rose, pink & light multicolored prints to frame the windmill effect; 100% Dacron batting. **$345.00**

409988 - *CENTER:* BUTTERFLIES; 81″ x 96″; orange & white; broadcloth & polyester/cotton; made in 1985 in Illinois;

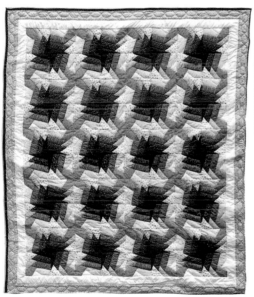

hand quilted; cross stitched orange butterflies set together with white broadcloth & orange with white dot of polyester & cotton. **$276.00**

509988 - *CENTER RIGHT:* REGENCY; 99″ x 99″; cotton percale print; hand quilted, cross stitched; flora strewn, domestic all cotton percale, cross stitched in two hues of ecru on eggshell. **$460.00**

609988 - *BOTTOM LEFT:* 9 PATCH; 84″ x 84″; multi-color; cotton; made in 1935 in New York; machine pieced, hand quilted; 9 multi-colored 9-patch squares surrounded by many colors forming a "checkerboard" wide border; unused; muslin backing. **$403.00**

709988 - *BOTTOM RIGHT:* NINE PATCH; 74″ x 76″; red, black & yellow; 100% cotton; made in 1950's in Pennsylvania; machine pieced, hand quilted; separate binding. **$288.00**

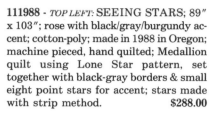

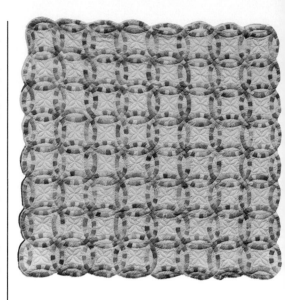

111988 - *TOP LEFT*: SEEING STARS; 89″ x 103″; rose with black/gray/burgundy accent; cotton-poly; made in 1988 in Oregon; machine pieced, hand quilted; Medallion quilt using Lone Star pattern, set together with black-gray borders & small eight point stars for accent; stars made with strip method. $288.00

211988 - *TOP RIGHT*: DOUBLE WEDDING RING; 101″ x 101″; cotton/polyester; made in 1988 in Missouri; machine pieced, hand quilted; multicolored with cream background, cotton/polyester, Dacron batting. $345.00

311988 - *CENTER LEFT*: 8 POINT STAR; 84″ x 104″; mauve, burgundy & white; cotton polyester; made in 1988 in Missouri; machine pieced, hand quilted. $317.00

411988 - *CENTER*: "FLIGHT BY NIGHT"; 76″ x 94″; cottons; made in 1987 in Minnesota; hand pieced, hand quilted; 20 original midwestern birds

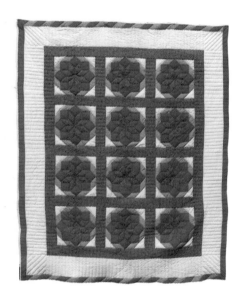

hand pieced in natural colors on pale gray backgrounds, green & black sashings. $863.00

511988 - *CENTER RIGHT*: ROYAL STAR OF ARIZONA; 90″ x 94″; cotton-polyester blend; made in 1988 in Missouri; machine pieced, hand quilted; royal blue & medium blue solid with navy & royal blue prints, background and lining are white; borders are medium blue print & solid. $345.00

611988 - *BOTTOM LEFT*: ROYAL STAR OF ALABAMA; 89″ x 98″; green prints, cream fill; cotton-polyester blend; made in 1988 in Missouri; machine pieced, hand quilted; made from dark green shaded to light green prints & solids of cotton-polyester; Dacron batting. $345.00

711988 - *BOTTOM RIGHT*: TIED SCRAPS; 100″ x 100″; multi-colored; velvet, silk, wool, cotton & polyester; made in 1977 in New York; machine pieced; random 5″ squares, hand tied. $345.00

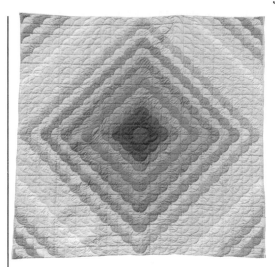

112988 - *TOP LEFT:* LONE STAR; 57″ x 57″; monochromatic green; cotton; made in 1985 in Minnesota; machine pieced, hand quilted; green "baby" Lone Star on pale green background, each diamond quilted, bows quilted into background, green pindot backing. **$115.00**

212988 - *TOP RIGHT:* LOVE RING; 96″ x 96″; rose & pink, cotton/polyester; made in 1988 in Missouri; machine pieced, hand quilted; made with center dark rose, shading out with each ring being lighter then back again to the dark rose prints & solids on the corners; Dacron batting. **$345.00**

312988 - *CENTER LEFT:* LONE STAR - 2 piece; 102″ x 102″; yellows-brown; cotton-poly; made in 1986 in Oregon; machine pieced, hand quilted; strip piecing method used for stars on the two piece (second piece not shown) queen size quilt, set together with unbleached muslin. **$345.00**

412988 - *CENTER:* PINWHEEL STAR; 75″ x 89″; mixed colors; cotton; made in

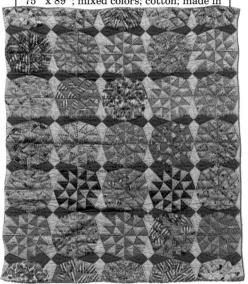

1945; quilt is a mixture of cotton prints connected by red/yellow stars. **$259.00**

512988 - *CENTER RIGHT:* WEATHER-VANE; 36″ x 36″; dark green print, dusty peach, cream; cotton; made in 1988 in Connecticut; machine pieced, hand quilted; wallhanging has an intricate quilting design on the inner 9 cream blocks. **$87.00**

612988 - *BOTTOM LEFT:* WINDMILL PRISMS; 30″ x 36″; multi-pastels; cotton & cotton blends; made in 1988 in Connecticut; machine pieced, hand quilted; Machine washable quilt with 5 different pastels, inside border has ostrich plume quilting design. **$115.00**

712988 - *BOTTOM RIGHT:* LOG CABIN; 81″ x 100″; wine & rose; cotton w/poly batt; made in 1985 in Kansas; machine pieced, hand quilted; 14″ Log Cabin blocks set in a star pattern, hand quilted by women of a Baptist church in Kansas. **$403.00**

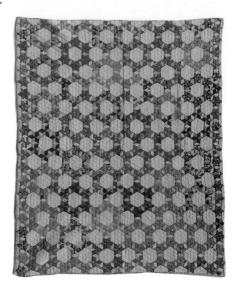

113988 - *TOP LEFT:* DIAMOND STAR; 65" x 78"; made in 1938 in Kentucky; hand pieced, hand quilted; this quilt is a mixture of colors of the 1930's; unusual design with colors blending well with each other; lightweight quilt. **$345.00**

213988 - *TOP RIGHT:* UNKNOWN; 50" x 72"; green & white; cotton; made in 1970's in Kentucky; hand embroidered, machine quilted; quilt has embroidered motifs on white blocks sashed with green gingham, framed with green cotton; muslin lining, polyester batting. Two of these are available for bunk beds. **$104.00**

313988 - *CENTER LEFT:* CENTER DIAMOND; 28" x 28"; pale pink, peach, cinnamon & brick red - all solid colors; 100% cotton, poly batting; made in 1987 in Massachusetts; hand pieced, hand quilted; hand quilted in matching color thread with Amish patterns. **$104.00**

413988 - *CENTER:* DIAGONAL TRIANGLES; 40" x 40"; pinks, red, purples, blues, greens alternating with black triangles, red inner border, black

outer border; 100% cottons, poly batting; made in 1987 in Massachusetts; hand pieced, hand quilted; all solid colors; hand quilted with black thread in traditional Amish patterns. **$144.00**

513988 - *CENTER RIGHT:* HAWAIIAN BREADFRUIT; 42" x 42"; brown & beige; 100% cotton with poly batting; made in 1983 in New York; hand quilted, hand appliqued; won 2nd place at New York State Fair, also won Best Quilting award at same show; some old, old Hawaiian quilts have cross hatching as shown on this. **$173.00**

613988 - *BOTTOM LEFT:* SUNRISE TAKEOFF; 24" x 36"; peaches, grays, golds, various pastels; 100% cottons; made in 1987 in New York; hand pieced, hand quilted; original design, juried at an art show in New York state & accepted to be hung. **$144.00**

713988 - *BOTTOM RIGHT:* DOUBLE IRISH CHAIN; 76" x 99"; hunter green, mint green, white; cotton w/poly batt; made in 1987 in Colorado; machine pieced, hand quilted; traditional pattern with original quilt design in plain blocks. **$460.00**

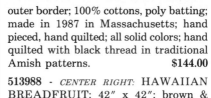

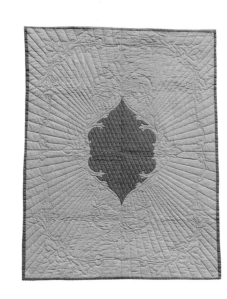

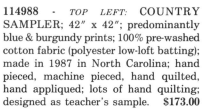

114988 - *TOP LEFT:* COUNTRY SAMPLER; 42″ x 42″; predominantly blue & burgundy prints; 100% pre-washed cotton fabric (polyester low-loft batting); made in 1987 in North Carolina; hand pieced, machine pieced, hand quilted, hand appliqued; lots of hand quilting; designed as teacher's sample. **$173.00**

214988 - *TOP RIGHT:* FLORIDA VICTORIAN; 38″ x 50″; light teal green & white; cotton; made in 1988 in Pennsylvania; hand quilted, hand appliqued; decorative design is quilted with teal colored thread on white fabric, filler quilt lines done in matching thread (white material/white thread), backing is light teal green. **$115.00**

314988 - *CENTER LEFT:* LOG CABIN – BARN RAISING; 60″ x 60″; navy & pink; cotton & cotton blends; made in 1982 in California; machine pieced, hand quilted; solid navy back. Never used. **$115.00**

414988 - *CENTER RIGHT:* COURTHOUSE STEPS W/BIRDS; 29″ x 42″; cream, gold, rust, green & blue; 100% cottons &

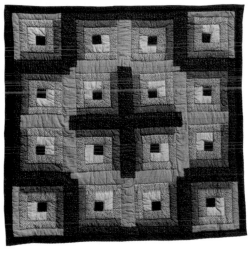

cotton/poly blends; made in 1987 in Washington; machine pieced, hand quilted; lo-loft batt; coordinated flower print back, quilted diagonal lines frame the birds while leaves on a vine coil through the border; birds are not appliqued, but rather part of the fabric. **$87.00**

514988 - *CENTER:* "EVERLASTING EVERGREEN"; 32½″ x 36½″; dark green & off-white; all 100% cottons; made in 1988 in Pennsylvania; machine pieced, hand quilted; variety of dark green prints machine pieced to create pine trees, extensive hand quilting. **$144.00**

614988 - *BOTTOM LEFT:* CHRISTMAS LONE STAR; 36″ x 36″; red & green; cotton, cotton & polyester; made in 1988 in Minnesota; hand pieced, hand quilted; star is pieced with red & green Christmas prints, quilting is a flower motif. **$104.00**

714988 - *BOTTOM RIGHT:* STAR LOG CABIN; 44″ x 44″; tones of blue with rust; cotton & polyester; made in 1987 in Illinois; machine pieced, hand quilted. **$110.00**

115988 - *TOP LEFT:* SWALLOWS IN FLIGHT; 33½″ x 33½″; yellows, green, brown, red, purple; front is 100% cottons & reverse is gingham (yellow & white); made in 1987 in Washington; machine pieced, hand quilted; quilting lines suggest circular pattern of flight, rod pockets at top & bottom for hanging, polyester lo-loft batt.   **$173.00**

215988 - *TOP RIGHT:* POTTED STAR FLOWER; 21″ x 63″; blues; cotton, cotton & polyester; made in 1987 in Minnesota; hand pieced, hand quilted; many different slate blue fabrics used in star flowers, intertwined quilting motif used in open spaces, ideal for hanging in open stairway.   **$110.00**

315988 - *CENTER LEFT:* AUTUMN WINDS; 38″ x 45″; tan, gold, rust & green; cottons & cotton blends; made in 1988 in North Dakota; machine pieced, machine quilted; represents the way the trees in the shelter-belts change color in

the fall, some are already brown & dead while some are still green; has twisting leaves quilted into the border.   **$52.00**

415988 - *CENTER:* FOUR PATCH VARIATION; 32″ x 32″; made in 1988 in Florida; hand quilted; stitching shows on the back.   **$52.00**

515988 - *CENTER RIGHT:* SUNSHINE & SHADOW; 37″ x 37″; Amish – purple, black, red & green; 100% cotton & cotton blends; made in 1988 in Florida; machine pieced, hand quilted binding, machine quilted.   **$87.00**

615988 - *BOTTOM LEFT:* LONE STAR WALLHANGING; 44″ x 44″; burgundy, polyester cotton & cotton; made in 1988 in Missouri; machine pieced, hand quilted.   **$115.00**

715988 - *BOTTOM RIGHT:* SUNBONNET SUE & FARMER BILL; 43″ x 52″; yellow check border; cotton/polyester; made in 1988 in Illinois; machine pieced, hand quilted, hand applique.   **$87.00**

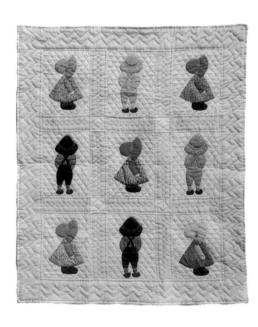

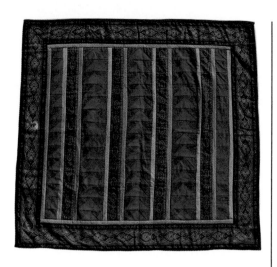

116988 - *TOP LEFT:* FLYING GEESE; 39" x 40½"; grays, rust; 100% cotton; made in 1988 in Florida; machine pieced, machine quilted; sleeve for hanging. $110.00

216988 - *TOP RIGHT:* ASTEROID STAR; hexagon 36" across; black, red, rust; cotton; made in 1987 in New Jersey; machine pieced, hand quilted. $230.00

316988 - *CENTER LEFT:* RAM IN THE GARDEN; 44" x 52"; smoke, mauve, green; imported & domestic silks & cottons; made in 1986 in Massachusetts; machine pieced, hand quilted; using as background a large muted floral print set in smoky black, pieced leaves in green, gold and mauve, sprinkled on rhinestones & embroidered silver dragon fly to give effect of garden strewn with leaves after a rain. $483.00

416988 - *CENTER:* CHILDREN OF THE WORLD; 24½" x 43"; multi-colored on

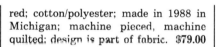

red; cotton/polyester; made in 1988 in Michigan; machine pieced, machine quilted; design is part of fabric. $79.00

516988 - *CENTER RIGHT:* SAFARI STAR; 39" x 39"; deep red, tan, navy; cotton blends, cotton classic batt; made in 1983 in North Dakota; machine pieced, hand quilted; center animals in stars are stuffed & background is stipple quilted; quilting motif in borders & sashing repeats figures in edges of peacock's tail. $144.00

616988 - *BOTTOM LEFT:* TEDDY BEARS; 33" x 41"; blue, plain & check, red dots; cotton & cotton with polyester; made in 1987 in Wisconsin; machine pieced, machine quilted, hand appliqued, hand embroidered; light blue backing, polyester fill. $75.00

716988 - *BOTTOM RIGHT:* LONE STAR; 78" x 96"; white with navy & red; cotton & polyester; made in 1987 in Illinois; machine pieced, hand quilted; early American look. $432.00

117988 - *TOP LEFT*: INDIAN LONE STAR; 39″ x 39″; reminiscent of Indian colors, gold, teal, rust & avocado; cottons; made in 1987 in Connecticut; machine pieced, hand quilted with repeating stars in the corners. **$173.00**

217988 - *TOP RIGHT*: NOVEMBER'S SONG, BAR QUILT; 47″ x 48″; rusts, browns, orange, purples, autumn flowers; cotton, blends, rayons; made in 1986 in California; machine pieced, hand quilted, hand embroidered; quilting is done with running stitch of embroidery floss; flannel sheeting instead of batting. **$259.00**

317988 - *CENTER LEFT*: MODIFIED LOG CABIN; octagon 35″ across; blue & rust; cotton; made in 1987 in New Jersey; machine pieced, hand quilted; maker adapted pattern into an octagon. **$173.00**

417988 - *CENTER*: SUNBONNET GIRL; 36″ x 43″; green (light & dark), red, yellow & blue; cotton, polyester blend; made in 1988 in Wisconsin; machine pieced, machine quilted, hand appliqued, hand

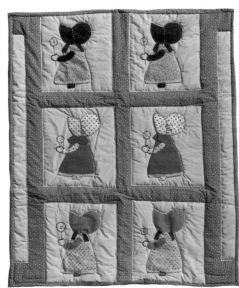

embroidered; polyester fill, light green backing. **$98.00**

517988 - *CENTER RIGHT*: "PIECES"; 26″ x 34″; solid blue borders with multicolored calico piecing, red, yellow, blue, beige, rust, green, mauve, lavender, white, etc.; cotton & cotton-polyester; made in 1986 in Colorado; machine pieced, hand quilted; strip-pieced from irregular strips. **$69.00**

617988 - *BOTTOM LEFT*: "ON WINGS"; 41″ x 42″; blue, greens, russets; cotton (some hand-dyed, tinted or bleached), nylon netting, embellished with miniature mother-of-pearl birds; made in 1986 in Massachusetts; hand & machine pieced, hand quilted; spring & fall aerial landscapes, with flocks of migrating, miniature birds. **$1,610.00**

717988 - *BOTTOM RIGHT*: SUNBONNET; 73″ x 86″; lavender & lavender print; cotton & polyester; made in 1987 in Indiana; machine quilted, hand appliqued. **$144.00**

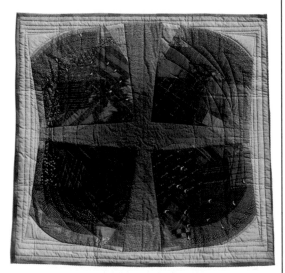

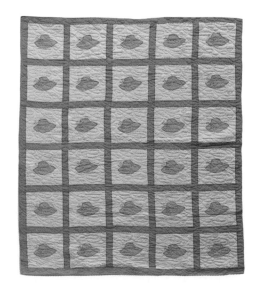

118988 - *TOP LEFT:* GOLDEN ANNIVER-SARY; 47″ x 47″; gold & white; pre-washed poly-blend cottons, polyester bat-ting; made in 1987 in Texas; machine piec-ed, hand quilted; painted with gold fabric paint & hand embroidered; wedding, an-niversary dates, names can be added; machine washable. $69.00

218988 - *TOP RIGHT:* CHOCOLATE MOUNTAINS; 38″ x 47″; brown/reds; 100% cotton; made in 1987 in Hawaii; machine pieced, hand quilted; cable quilting around border, some hand-dyed fabrics, bonded poly batting, double bias binding. $202.00

318988 - *CENTER LEFT:* DOUBLE IRISH CHAIN; 40″ x 40″; green, red & ivory; made in 1987 in Connecticut; machine pieced, hand quilted & appliqued; corner blocks in the plain blocks were hand ap-pliqued so that the teddy bear print would not be cut & distorted when piecing the plain blocks. $87.00

418988 - *CENTER:* CENTERING – IN SEARCH OF; 30″ x 48″; reds, pink, greens; cotton & blends; made in 1983 in California; hand pieced, hand quilted; us-ed vibrant colors to expand the tumbling block pattern, when hanging gives the il-lusion that it is dimensional. $403.00

518988 - *CENTER RIGHT:* CAROLINA LI-LY; 41″ x 41″; off-white, muted red & green; 100% cotton; made in 1987 in New York; machine pieced, hand quilted; pre-washed cottons, reds & greens on muslin, stuffed work on borders. $230.00

618988 - *BOTTOM LEFT:* ROCKY HORSE; 40″ x 45″; blue, yellow & brown; cotton & polyester; made in Texas; hand pieced, hand quilted. $69.00

718988 - *BOTTOM RIGHT:* LOG CABIN; 76″ x 96″; blue; cotton & polyester; made in 1985 in Indiana; machine pieced, machine quilted. $115.00

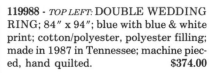

119988 - *TOP LEFT:* DOUBLE WEDDING RING; 84″ x 94″; blue with blue & white print; cotton/polyester, polyester filling; made in 1987 in Tennessee; machine pieced, hand quilted. **$374.00**

219988 - *TOP RIGHT:* FANCY FAN; 86″ x 106″; off-white, dusty pink with dusty pink & gray print; cotton/polyester; made in 1987 in Tennessee; machine pieced, hand quilted. **$489.00**

319988 - *CENTER LEFT:* GARDEN WALL; 80″ x 98″; soft greens & floral shades; cotton; made in California; hand pieced, hand quilted; all fabrics used are pre-shrunk & dye-set; Amish quilter. **$432.00**

419988 - *CENTER:* MEXICAN ROSE; 74″ x 102″; rust & browns; cotton; made in 1980 in California; hand pieced, hand quilted. **$432.00**

519988 - *CENTER RIGHT:* LONE STAR; 91″ x 91″; green; cottons & blends; made in 1988 in Utah; all fabrics have been prewashed. **$460.00**

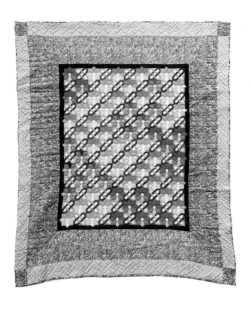

619988 - *BOTTOM LEFT:* "DELECTABLE MOUNTAINS" VARIATION; 71″ x 72″; solids of medium orange & pale yellow; cotton; made c. 1925; machine pieced, hand quilted; quilt is covered with lots of quilting in concentric circles. **$432.00**

719988 - *BOTTOM RIGHT:* "DOUBLE WEDDING RING"; 71″ x 78″; multiprints & solids on a lavender background; cotton; made c. 1935 in Ohio; machine pieced, hand quilted; color combination is unusual but works well. **$213.00**

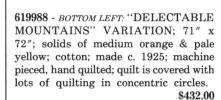

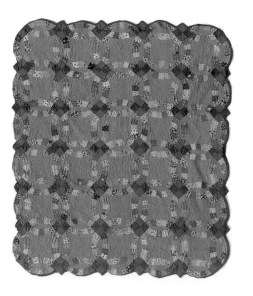

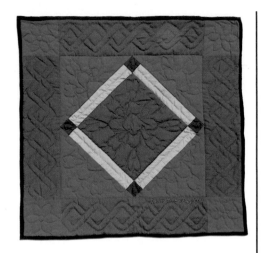

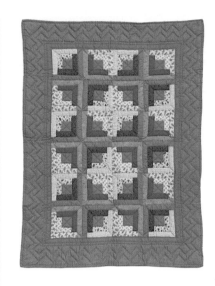

1011288 - *TOP LEFT:* AMISH DIAMOND; 26" x 26"; blues, purples, violet & black; cottons with bonded poly batting; made in Virginia in 1986; machine pieced, hand quilted; quilting teacher's class sample using authentic Amish colors/fabrics; quilting patterns of cables, pumpkin seeds, etc; quilting in black thread on black backing. $81.00

2011288 - *TOP RIGHT:* LOG CABIN CRIB; 35" x 47"; rose; cotton/polyester; made in Illinois in 1988; machine pieced, hand quilted; this quilt is great for baby girl, also lovely wallhanging or table centerpiece. $75.00

3011288 - *CENTER LEFT:* STARLIT NIGHT; 29" x 29", muslin, blues, purples, metallics; front is 100% preshrunk cotton plus metallics, back is cotton/poly; made in Washington in 1988; machine pieced, hand quilted; Starlit night sky shines through attic windows. $92.00

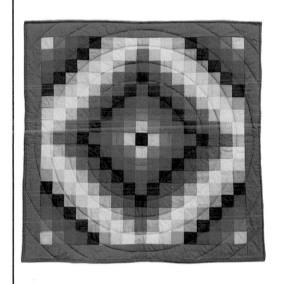

4011288 – *CENTER:* POSTAGE STAMP; 67" x 82"; cotton; made in Tennessee in 1945; hand pieced, hand quilted; quilted in fans & made up of hundreds of 1⅛" squares of mixed colors, red & navy being predominant. $460.00

5011288 – *CENTER RIGHT:* SUPERNOVA; 38" x 38"; blues, purples, melons; front is 100% preshrunk cotton & back is cotton/poly; made in Washington in 1988; machine pieced, hand quilted; circular quilting sets squares in motion. $156.00

6011288 – *BOTTOM LEFT:* CUBE ACCENT; 42" x 42"; blue; cotton polyester; made in Missouri in 1988; hand & machine pieced, hand quilted; made with blue print & royal blue solid; 100% polyester batting. $70.00

7011288 – *BOTTOM RIGHT:* MODERN SEMINOLE; 40" x 47"; black, red & gray Seminole stripwork; 100% cotton; made in California in 1985; machine pieced, machine quilted; Seminole stripwork made as a window quilt to brighten a drafty corner window in the maker's previous residence. $60.00

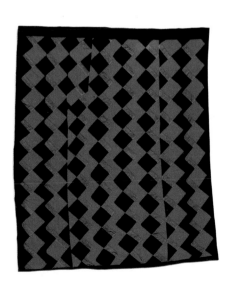

1021288 – *TOP LEFT:* OAK LEAF; 28" x 28"; brown & off-white; cotton, cotton & polyester; made in Minnesota in 1986; hand pieced; hand quilted; hand appliqued; suitable for wallhanging, table cover or bed topper, antique-look brown & gold paisley on off-white muslin, machine wash & dry. $70.00

2021288 – *TOP RIGHT:* AMISH DIAMOND; 27" x 27"; blues, violets, purples, black; cottons purchased in Amish store, bonded poly batting; made in Virginia in 1986; machine pieced, hand quilted; teacher's sample using authentic Amish colors/fabric; fine stitches with black thread, black backing. $92.00

3021288 – *CENTER LEFT:* FLOWERING FERN; 34" x 34"; red & green; cotton, cotton & polyester; made in Minnesota in 1986; hand quilted, hand appliqued; very old pattern, antique-looking red & green fabrics, machine wash & dry. $92.00

4021288 – *CENTER:* LOG CABIN; 70½" x 91"; multi-color; satin & satin blends; made in Tennessee in 1988; hand pieced, hand quilted; quilted by the piece & made up of dark blue, rose, burgundy, beige, light blue & pink with a blue border. $345.00

5021288 – *CENTER RIGHT:* LOG CABIN; 44" x 44"; multi-colored with navy center; cotton/polyester; made in Missouri in 1988; machine pieced, hand quilted. $65.00

6021288 – *BOTTOM LEFT:* ENTHUSIASM!; 24" x 31½"; turquoise, white & pink; solid cottons; made in Connecticut in 1988; design is machine pieced then hand appliqued onto the background; background as well as the pieced design are fully hand quilted. $98.00

7021288 – *BOTTOM RIGHT:* RADICAL ENERGY; 24" x 26½"; black, rose, sapphire blue; solid cotton & cotton blends; made in Connecticut in 1988; machine pieced, hand quilted; the maker used crazy quilt technique then cut it into strips; to give it a sense of control she pieced it with solid black strips. $87.00

1041288 – *TOP LEFT:* DECK THE HALLS AND ALL THAT JAZZ (combination of 9-Patch & variation of Snow Ball); 57" x 57"; red, white & green; cottons & blends; made in California in 1986; machine pieced, hand quilted; quilted in the ditch; polyester traditional batting; inspired by workshop on using two patterns & then mirror imaging. $633.00

2041288 – *TOP RIGHT:* ONCE UPON A TIME; 33" x 33"; blacks, deep cranberries; made in California in 1985; hand pieced, machine pieced, embroidered, beaded, appliqued, minimal quilting; in the quilt are gifts from friends of metallic braid from Germany, rayon velveteen from a Navaho friend, French moire ribbon, antique fabrics, handpainted silks, scraps of polyester, bound with scraps from an old rayon petticoat & lined with a patched piece of a silk sari. $432.00

3041288 – *CENTER LEFT:* BASKET OF LILIES; 27½" x 35½"; blues & lavenders; 100% cotton;

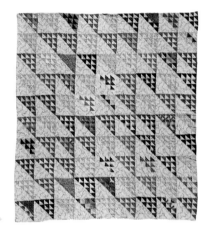

made in Hawaii in 1985; machine pieced, hand quilted; enlarged from book by E. Porter & M. Fons; quilt never used. $115.00

4041288 – *CENTER:* LADY OF THE LAKE; 80" x 91"; multi-color; cotton; made in Kentucky in 1935; hand pieced, hand quilted; quilted in fans, varied colors with gray predominating. $489.00

5041288 – *CENTER RIGHT:* LOG CABIN; 44" x 44"; Multi-color with medium blue center; cotton/polyester; made in Missouri in 1988; machine pieced, hand quilted; 100% polyester fill. $65.00

6041288 – *BOTTOM LEFT:* LONE STAR; 43" x 43"; blue; cotton-polyester; made in Missouri in 1988; machine pieced, hand quilted. $87.00

7041288 – *BOTTOM RIGHT:* LOVER'S KNOT; 56" x 56"; cream, antique berry & green; 100% top quality cottons, prewashed; made in Colorado in 1987; machine pieced, hand quilted; wallhanging with hearts in the printed fabric & in the quilting motifs; has an aged look. $196.00

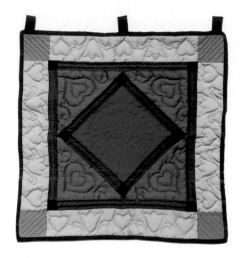

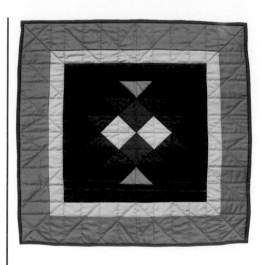

1051288 – *TOP LEFT:* CENTER DIAMOND; 26" x 26"; Amish colors; cotton/poly; made in Missouri in 1988; machine pieced, hand quilted; Amish colors. $70.00

2051288 – *TOP RIGHT:* AN AMISH MOUNTAIN, 24" x 24", violet, indigo, lavender, plum, wine & pink with light blue & sky blue borders; 100% cotton & cotton sateen, cotton batting; made in Missouri in 1987; machine pieced, hand quilted; exhibited in the Corridors Gallery & Stone House Gallery. $115.00

3051288 – *CENTER LEFT:* CHRISTMAS CANDLE WALLHANGING; 31" x 31"; Christmas prints & solids; cotton; made in Pennsylvania in 1988; machine pieced, hand quilted; appliqued red candle, gold flame & green holly leaves on natural background. Log Cabin strips of red & green Christmas prints. Solid green border; backing is a Christmas print. $133.00

4051288 – *CENTER:* DOUBLE IRISH CHAIN; 82" x 102"; blue & white; all cotton; made in 1980; machine pieced, hand appliqued & quilted; pattern from an Aunt Martha's quilt book. $426.00

5051288 – *CENTER RIGHT:* LOG CABIN; 35" x 46"; prints, pink, blue lining; cotton-poly; made in Kentucky in 1986; hand pieced, hand quilted; crib quilt or wallhanging, very old fashioned prints; colors are good for boy or girl & fit a country theme. $87.00

6051288 – *BOTTOM LEFT:* OZARK MIDNIGHT; 36" x 36"; wine, violet, plum, gray, light jade & turquoise; 100% cotton & polished cotton, cotton batting; made in Missouri in 1987; machine pieced, hand quilted; wallhanging represents the Ozark Mountains seen while sailing on the Lake of the Ozarks late one evening. $156.00

7051288 – *BOTTOM RIGHT:* ROMAN STRIPES; 84½" x 100"; bright Amish colors on black; 100% prewashed cotton; made in Illinois in 1988; machine pieced, hand quilted; traditional Amish quilt made entirely out of solids, six bright, bold colors shine against a black background, intricately quilted using black thread on black, colored thread on the colors, black back. $460.00

43

1061288 – *TOP LEFT:* RADIANT NINE PATCH; 82" x 98"; blues, grays, maroons, pinks; cotton & cotton blends; made in Utah in 1988; machine pieced, machine quilted; all new, prewashed fabrics. $230.00.

2061288 – *TOP RIGHT:* STAR OVER FLORIDA; 84" x 100"; multi-colored prints & muslin; 100% prewashed cotton; made in Illinois in 1988; machine pieced, hand quilted; multi-colored calico prints in country colors with muslin; muslin back, Mountain Mist batting. $405.00

3061288 – *CENTER LEFT:* DRUNKARD'S PATH; 82" x 100"; red & white; cotton; made in 1988; hand pieced, hand quilted. $345.00

4061288 – *CENTER:* TULIP; 71½" x 88½"; red, beige; satin; made in Tennessee in 1987; hand quilted, hand appliqued; quilted tulips in the beige corners. $375.00

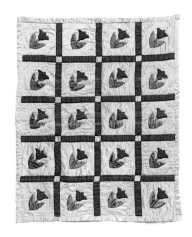

5061288 – *CENTER RIGHT:* SUNBONNET GIRL; 38" x 47"; red & white hearts & bows; white sunbonnet girl; cotton & cotton blends; made in Wisconsin in 1988; machine pieced, machine quilted, hand embroidered. $70.00

6061288 – *BOTTOM LEFT:* FAN; 81" x 103"; blues, grays, maroons & pinks; cotton & cotton blends; made in Utah in 1988; machine pieced, hand quilted; variation of Grandmother's Fan, all new, prewashed fabrics, won "Sweepstakes" at county fair, signed & dated. $435.00

7061288 – *BOTTOM RIGHT:* ALABAMA; 84" x 108"; brown, peach & cream; 100% prewashed cotton; made in Alabama in 1988; machine pieced, hand quilted; muslin back, Mountain Mist batting. $435.00

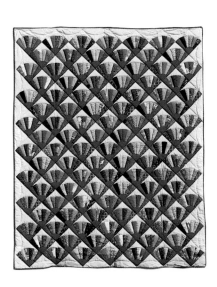

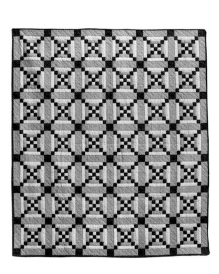

44

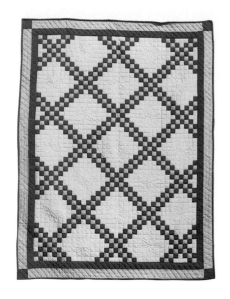

1071288 – *TOP LEFT:* DOUBLE IRISH CHAIN; 82" x 110"; blue/white; 100% prewashed cotton; made in Illinois in 1987; machine pieced, hand quilted; delicate blue, white print, blue pin dot & muslin, with a muslin back, Mountain Mist batting. $405.00

2071288 – *TOP RIGHT:* TULIP; 76" x 80"; green, pink, beige; cotton; made in Kentucky in 1943; hand pieced, hand quilted; beautiful tulip tree done in pink, beige & green cotton material with pink & white border. $405.00

3071288 – *CENTER LEFT:* COLONIAL GARDEN; 86" x 92"; multi-colored flowers set with yellow, dark blue binding with white backing; cotton blends; made in Kentucky in 1988; hand pieced, hand quilted; quilted by the piece; polyester batting. $260.00

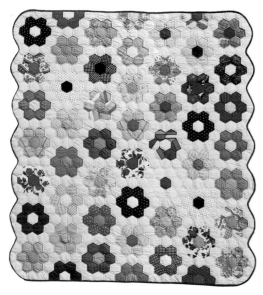

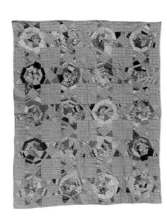

4071288 – *CENTER:* 8 POINT STRING STAR; 63½" x 73"; multi-colored with beige; cotton; made in Tennessee c. 1950; hand pieced, hand quilted; neatly quilted lightweight quilt with a medium beige background, various prints & solids. $345.00

5071288 – *CENTER RIGHT:* SCRAP QUILT; 74" x 89½"; machine pieced, hand quilted; made in Tennessee; won 2nd place in the Arts & Craft Show at the 1987 Peach Festival in Brownsville, TN. $405.00

6071288 – *BOTTOM LEFT:* CALICO WREATH; 82" x 100"; peach; cotton; made in 1988; hand quilted, hand appliqued. $345.00

7071288 – *BOTTOM RIGHT:* PINK LIGHTNING; 70" x 90"; dark forest green, pink, peach; 100% cotton both sides; 100% polyester batting; made in California in 1987; machine pieced, machine quilted; rich dark forest green calico & two bright pinks with a touch of peach. $605.00

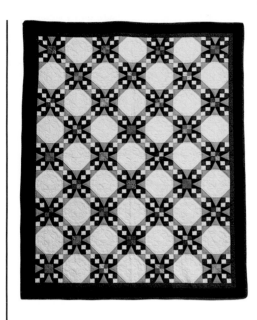

1081288 – *TOP LEFT:* BOW TIE; 70" x 77"; variegated colors; cotton blends; made in Kentucky in 1988; hand pieced, hand quilted; quilted close by the piece; polyester batting, very soft & puffy. $175.00

2081288 – *TOP RIGHT:* TENNESSEE WALTZ; 71" x 90"; burgundy, black, tan with colored centers; 100% prewashed cotton; made in Illinois in 1987; machine pieced, hand quilted; multi-colored calico squares contrast with black star points & show up against the tan print & shine, intricately quilted with a muslin back. $391.00

3081288 – *CENTER LEFT:* BEAR'S PAW; 76" x 84½"; multi-color yellow & brown; cottons & cotton/polyester blend; made in New York in 1988; hand pieced, hand quilted; pattern copied from a quilt magazine using scraps of material, all new; won a third place ribbon. $345.00

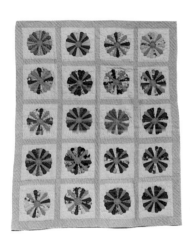

4081288 – *CENTER:* DRESDEN PLATE; 74" x 88"; light blue with multi-prints; cotton-poly; made in Kentucky in 1987; hand pieced, hand quilted; pastel colors lined in white, lots of quilting, hearts quilted in each corner of block. $320.00

5081288 – *CENTER RIGHT:* SIMPLY ELEGANT; 56" x 56"; earth tones with gold; cotton/polyester; made in Illinois in 1988; hand pieced, machine pieced, hand quilted; use as tablecloth to fit 45" round table or wallhanging, made with yo-yo flowers appliqued & tiny squares of patchwork. $410.00

6081288 – *BOTTOM LEFT:* A VERY SPECIAL WHIG ROSE; 86" x 104"; off-white, navy, light & dark rose & print; 100% cotton; made in Wisconsin in 1988; hand quilted, hand appliqued. $589.00

7081288 – *BOTTOM RIGHT:* COUNTRY BARN RAISING; 80" x 98"; navy, burgundy, cream colors; 100% cotton front & back, 100% polyester batting, very thick; made in California in 1988; machine pieced, machine quilted; back is covered in navy & antique white fabric called "Matrimony"; scenes of courtship, doves & flowers. $605.00

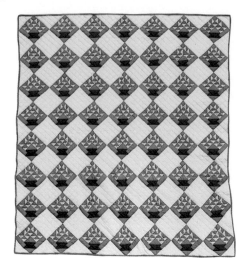

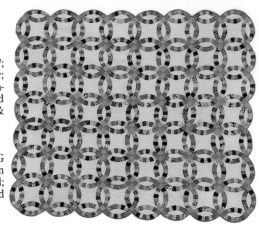

1091288 – *TOP LEFT:* MAY BASKET; 80" x 90"; beige, green, brown & yellow print; cotton/poly; made in Missouri in 1986; hand quilted, machine pieced; block pieced in green background with yellow print & brown, beige plain blocks & lining. $230.00

2091288 – *TOP RIGHT:* DOUBLE WEDDING RING; 84" x 95"; multi-colored; cotton; made in Kentucky in 1935; hand pieced, hand quilted; done in many antique colors of print; hand bound in green. $435.00

3091288 *CENTER LEFT:* BLUE STAR; 80" x 80"; navy blue on off-white; cotton; made in Illinois; has old navy blue prints (antique), put together with off-white feed sacks, old top but quilted in 1986, "rusty" looking but never been used. $299.00

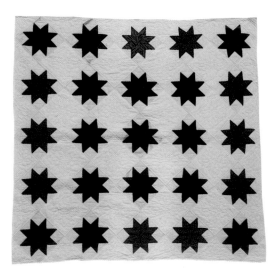

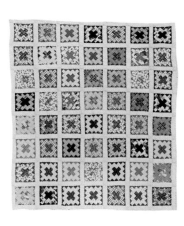

4091288 – *CENTER:* CHURN DASH; 74" x 84"; multi-cotton prints & off-white lining; cotton blends; made in Kentucky; hand pieced, hand quilted; top made in 1932 & was quilted in 1986; many stitches, very country & old fashioned; the quilter pieced the top when she was 10 years old. $288.00

5091288 – *CENTER RIGHT:* A FIELD OF LILIES; 78" x 88"; yellow & gold with green; all new cotton & domestic material with Mountain Mist cotton batting; made in Kentucky in 1935; border was sewed on by machine, but rest was hand pieced & hand quilted. $317.00

6091288 – *BOTTOM LEFT:* AROUND THE WORLD; 69" x 77"; multi-colored; all new cotton print & muslin lining, cotton batting; made in 1939; hand pieced, hand quilted except for machine sewn border. $230.00

7091288 – *BOTTOM RIGHT:* SAILBOAT; 34" x 42"; cotton & poly/cottons; made in Wisconsin in 1988; machine pieced, machine quilted, hand embroidered; polyester batting; comes with a pillow. $60.00

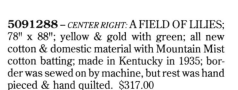

1101288 – *TOP LEFT:* LOG CABIN; 68½" x 81½"; multi-colored; cotton; made in Kentucky c. 1940; hand pieced, hand quilted; many different colored pieces of fabric comprise this quilt, red, blue & yellow being the center block. $575.00

2101288 – *TOP RIGHT:* CASTLE WALL MEDALLION; 79" x 96"; peach, browns, turquoise; cottons; made in New York in 1984; hand quilted, machine pieced; elongated central castle wall block is surrounded by borders and castle wall blocks set on point. $345.00

3101288 – *CENTER LEFT:* DRESDEN PLATE; 70" x 88"; blue; cotton/polyester blend; made in Philippines in 1987; machine pieced, hand quilted. $288.00

4101288 – *CENTER:* FLOWER GARDEN; 72" x 86"; 100% cotton fabrics; made in Illinois in 1977;

hand pieced, hand quilted; over 2,500 hexagons used in piecing this pink, lavender, peach & green. Quilting was done by going around each seam of all hexagons. $345.00

5101288 – *CENTER RIGHT:* BARBARA FRITCHIE'S STAR; 72" x 84"; gold, cranberry, royal blue solids with VIP med. blue print containing above colors & unbleached muslin; cotton & cotton/poly 50/50, batting is Kodel Dacron; made in Arkansas in 1986; machine pieced, hand quilted; quilted with thread to match solids in top; backing white with small medium blue floral; all colors dyeset, very soft feeling fabrics. $196.00

6101288 – *BOTTOM LEFT:* UNTITLED; 95" x 101"; rose/blue; cotton polyester blend; made in Philippines; machine pieced, hand quilted. $345.00

7101288 – *BOTTOM RIGHT:* SPLIT RAIL FENCE; 68" x 82"; multi-colored with red back; cotton; made in Virginia in 1932; hand pieced, hand quilted. $115.00

48

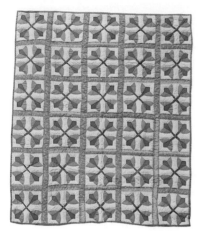

1111288 – *TOP LEFT:* TULIP; 70" x 82"; colonial blue, rust, green stems on white; cotton/poly; made in Kentucky in 1988; hand pieced, hand quilted, hand appliqued; strips of light & medium blue print & lined in colonial blue. Hi-loft batting make tulips puffed. $288.00

2111288 – *TOP RIGHT:* TRIP AROUND THE WORLD; 75" x 95"; burgundy & blue with white; top & back polyester & cotton, batting is polyester; made in California in 1988; machine pieced, hand quilted; all new fabric. $345.00

3111288 – *CENTER LEFT:* JOY TO THE WORLD, 53" x 70"; blues (sky), various colored buildings; cottons; made in New York in 1985; hand quilted, machine pieced; Bethlehem star is shining over the modern city; design adapted from a Christmas card. $288.00

4111288 – *CENTER:* COUNTRY JAMBOREE; 63" x 87"; yellow, brown, rust with multi-colors; cotton/poly blends; made in Washington in 1987; hand pieced, hand quilted; done in warm, summer/fall colors. $259.00

5111288 – *CENTER RIGHT:* T SQUARE; 66" x 78"; red & white; cotton; made in North Carolina in 1940's; hand pieced, hand quilted; striking red & white quilt with a nice design. $345.00

6111288 – *BOTTOM LEFT:* BUTTERFLY; 77" x 94"; multi-colored butterflies; red prints & calicoes; cotton & cotton blends; made in California in 1986; hand quilted, machine appliqued; good quality quilting. $405.00

7111288 – *BOTTOM RIGHT:* WINTERLUDE; 78" x 95"; greens & lavenders; cotton; made in California in 1983; hand pieced, hand quilted; lavender backing. $405.00

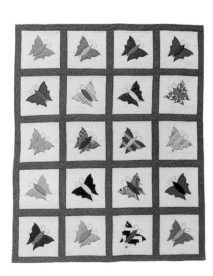

1121288 – *TOP LEFT:* ATTIC WINDOWS; 78" x 91"; cream, light rust solid & print, brown & white gingham; perma-press; made in Tennessee in 1986; machine pieced, hand quilted; really looks like "attic windows," edged with "prairie points"; perfect for boy's room. $230.00

2121288 – *TOP RIGHT:* FOUR SQUARE; 79" x 95"; gold & multi-colored; cotton; made in California in 1986; hand pieced, hand quilted; Amish quilted, Indian orange backing, nearly 400 different fabrics used. $405.00

3121288 – *CENTER LEFT:* ROYAL STAR OF PENNSYLVANIA; 88" x 96"; royal & light blue solids & prints & white; cotton/poly blend; made in Missouri in 1988; hand quilted, machine pieced; one of the series of Royal Stars of the States designed by Eula Long; 100% Dacron batting. $345.00

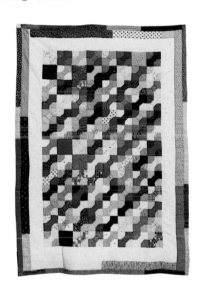

4121288 – *CENTER:* BOW TIE; 74" x 106"; multi-color; cotton & polyester fabric; made in Georgia in 1987; machine pieced, hand quilted with machine embroidery. $175.00

5121288 – *CENTER RIGHT:* DOUBLE X; 73" x 82"; blue, red & blond; cotton; made in Pennsylvania c. 1910; hand pieced, hand quilted; homespun navy plaid back, cotton. $519.00

6121288 – *BOTTOM LEFT:* IRISH CHAIN; 64" x 83"; red, green & ivory; cotton; made in Pennsylvania c. 1900; hand pieced, hand quilted. $445.00

7121288 – *BOTTOM RIGHT:* NINE PATCH; 75" X 83"; rose, brown calico prints; cotton; made in Pennsylvania c. 1880; hand pieced, hand quilted. $449.00

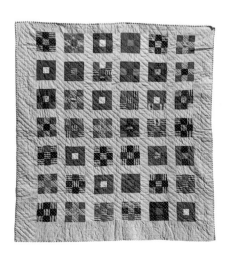

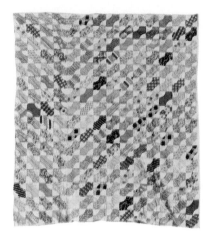

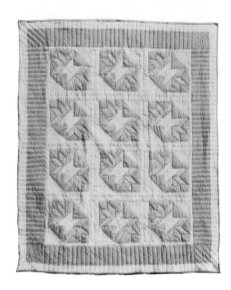

1131288 – *TOP LEFT:* VARIATION OF "BOSTON"; 72" x 82"; scrap blues, pinks, greens; cotton, 1930's & 1940's prints; made in North Carolina in 1940's; hand pieced, hand quilted; some printed feed sacks & some white feed sacks in top; four white feed sacks on back. $299.00

2131288 – *TOP RIGHT:* QUEEN CHARLOTTE'S CROWN; 78" x 96"; lavender & white; cotton/poly; made in Missouri in 1986; hand quilted, machine pieced; pieced solid white & lavender with lavender plaid, lavender lining. $230.00

3131288 – *CENTER LEFT:* ROYAL STAR OF KANSAS; 85" x 89"; cream, blue & coral; cotton; made in Indiana in 1988; machine pieced, hand quilted; 7-9 stitches per inch, bias bound, fits double bed with a foot board, signed & dated, muslin (unbleached) back. $519.00

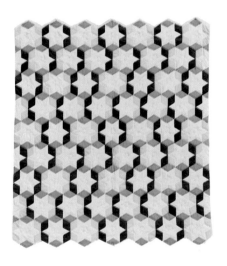

4131288 – *CENTER:* "HOE WA' A" - CANOE PADDLERS; 47" x 72"; gypsy red applique on bronco background; applique & background is Imperial Broadcloth, quilt backing is VIP Calico; made in Marshall Islands in 1987; hand quilted, hand appliqued; quilt design depicts canoe warriors of legendary Hawaii, machine wash & dry; echo quilting ½" rows. $782.00

5131288 – *CENTER RIGHT:* TUMBLING BLOCK; 77" x 90"; green; cotton/poly; made in Pennsylvania in 1973; machine pieced, hand quilted; dark, medium to light green, white back & background. $230.00

6131288 – *BOTTOM LEFT:* KANSAS DUGOUT; 76" x 88"; variety of colors; mostly cotton feedsacks; made in Arkansas; hand pieced, hand quilted; lean times 1930's quilt. $230.00

7131288 – *BOTTOM RIGHT:* LONE STAR; 66" x 66"; dusty rose/black; cotton; made in Indiana in 1987; machine pieced, hand quilted; can be wallhanging, nap quilt or will fit on twin size bed with foot board; 7-8 stitches per inch. $288.00

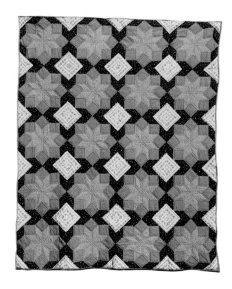

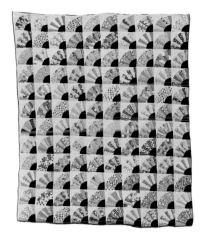

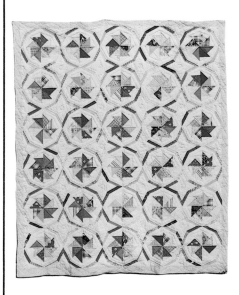

1141288 – *TOP LEFT:* TUMBLIN' STAR; 83" x 105"; blue on blue; cotton & cotton blends made in Alabama in 1988; hand quilted, machine pieced; sheet lining, double quilted. $288.00

2141288 – *TOP RIGHT:* TRIALS AND TROUBLES; 87" x 92"; blues, shades of pink & rose; cotton broadcloth & blends; made in Arkansas in 1988; hand quilted, machine pieced; can be called scrap or string quilt; quilted around each seam, cotton blend backing & polyester batting, variegated prints. $230.00

3141288 – *CENTER LEFT:* LONE STAR; 96" x 98"; multi-colored; cotton; made in Alabama in 1988; machine pieced, hand quilted. $405.00

4141288 – *CENTER:* FAN; 63½" x 73"; multi-color, navy; cotton; made in Tennessee; hand pieced, hand quilted; muslin backing. $288.00

5141288 – *CENTER RIGHT:* BOW TIE; 85" x 97"; blue & brown; cotton; made in Arkansas in 1987; hand & machine pieced; hand quilted; solid blocks & print with nice quilting. $230.00

6141288 – *BOTTOM LEFT:* TRIP AROUND THE WORLD, 86" x 87"; multi-color plains & prints with pink border & backing; cotton; made in California in 1986; machine pieced, hand quilted; small quilting stitch. $405.00

7141288 – *BOTTOM RIGHT:* WHEEL OF FORTUNE; 86" x 102"; multi-prints, beige cotton blend; cotton & cotton blends; made in Arkansas in 1987; machine pieced, hand quilted; wheel is of cotton & blends, polyester batting, quilted around each seam. $230.00

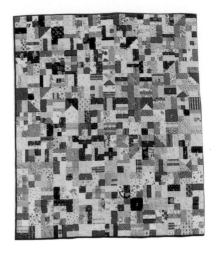

1151288 – *TOP LEFT:* MANY PIECES; 75" x 90"; multi-colored prints; cotton, cotton-polyester blends; made in North Carolina in 1988; machine pieced, tied; old fashioned look achieved with variety of pre-washed fabrics, dark blue cotton backing; unused. $230.00

2151288– *TOP RIGHT:* ROYAL STAR OF MARYLAND; 88" x 96"; brown & rust solids & prints; cotton/poly blend; made in Missouri in 1988; machine pieced, hand quilted; made with small center star with larger points to form the complete star in shades of rust & brown with cream fill & lining, 100% Dacron batting. $345.00

3151288 – *CENTER LEFT:* LOG CABIN; 102" x 117"; beige, brown & pink; poly/cotton blend; made in Illinois in 1987; machine pieced, hand quilted; pillow included. $242.00

4151288 – *CENTER:* OHIO STAR; 76" x 80"; yellow calico with prints; calico with printed cottons; made in Pennsylvania in 1930; hand pieced; hand quilted; thick & warm. $405.00

5151288 – *CENTER RIGHT:* STARS AND BARS; 70" x 74"; light, medium & dark solids; cotton/poly, all new fabrics; made in Arkansas in 1988; machine pieced, machine quilted; navy blue solid back, Amish-type quilting with navy thread in scroll pattern; quilt has been washed (fabrics are dye-set), Kodel "88" Dacron batting. $138.00

6151288 – *BOTTOM LEFT:* BUTTERFLIES; 78" X 92"; multi-color butterflies on white muslin blocks, soft green sashing & back; cottons, polyester batting; hand quilted, hand appliqued; butterflies showcase marvelous 1930's & 1940's prints; 1st place award applique quilt, 1986 Albion, PA fair, judge's critique: "excellent color in sashing, lovely, fine stitches;" excellent condition, a few age spots on blocks. $405.00

7151288 – *BOTTOM RIGHT:* SQUARE IN THE MIDDLE; 86" x 100"; mauve, off-white; cotton, polyester blend; made in Minnesota in 1988; machine pieced, hand quilted; quilt is country design enhanced by hearts quilted throughout; back of quilt is mauve. $405.00

1161288 – *TOP LEFT:* LONE STAR; 112" x 112"; blue & white; cotton; made in Kentucky in 1988; machine pieced, hand quilted; king-size quilt (wrinkled in photo only). $345.00

2161288 – *TOP RIGHT:* LOG CABIN; 100" x 100"; purple, rose, blue, beige, brown, yellow; paisley cotton; made in Tennessee in 1982; machine pieced, hand quilted; different color prints. $345.00

3161288 – *CENTER LEFT:* LOG CABIN; 100" x 116"; polyester; made in Illinois in 1988; machine pieced, hand quilted. $230.00

4161288 – *CENTER:* SCHOOLHOUSE; 86" x 106"; blue & white; all cotton; made in Kentucky in 1988; hand pieced, hand quilted. $345.00

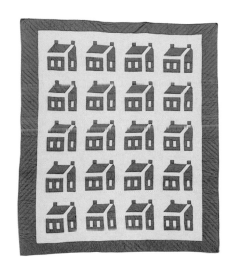

5161288 – *CENTER RIGHT:* LOG CABIN; 62" x 74"; all colors; wool; made in Tennessee in 1986; machine pieced, tied; wool log cabin with scarlet centers & prairie points; would make a great wall quilt in country decorating scheme. $230.00

6161288 – *BOTTOM LEFT:* IRIS TIME IN TENNESSEE; 77½" x 96½"; "Iris" colors, lavender, purple, etc.; all 100% cotton; made in Tennessee in 1988; hand quilted, hand appliqued; Iris is state flower of Tennessee; washable. $575.00

7161288 – *BOTTOM RIGHT:* MARINER'S COMPASS; 79" x 95"; white background with blue, rust & floral print; 100% cotton; made in Delaware in 1988; machine pieced, hand quilted; 100% polyester batting, hand quilted by Amish lady. $690.00

54

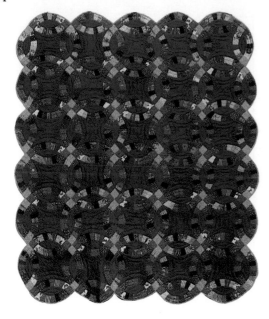

1171288 – *TOP LEFT:* WEDDING RING; 96" x 108"; brown; poly/cotton blend; made in Illinois in 1988; machine pieced, hand quilted. $259.00

2171288 – *TOP RIGHT:* LILY MEDALLION; 96" x 106"; pinks, mauves, maroon & green on eggshell; cotton & cotton blends; made in New York in 1987; machine pieced, hand quilted; Carolina Lily design medallion in field of borders with outermost border comprised of "string" hearts & swag, quality hand quilting throughout. $805.00

3171288 – *CENTER LEFT:* LONE STAR; 94" x 100"; blue; cotton polyester; made in Missouri in 1988; machine pieced, hand quilted; polyester fill. $345.00

4171288 – *CENTER:* ALBUM; 67½" x 75"; mixed; cotton; made in Tennessee in 1955; hand pieced, hand quilted; quilted in rectangles on a muslin background; lightweight. $345.00

5171288 – *CENTER RIGHT:* AMISH SHADOWS; 76" x 86"; cotton & cotton blend; made in Missouri in 1987; machine pieced, hand quilted; Amish-style quilt with feather design quilting, solid colors in black & burgundies create a striking contemporary look; the back is black, as well as the quilting thread. $575.00

6171288 – *BOTTOM LEFT:* HEART QUILT; 114" x 141"; white; cotton & polyester; hand quilted; made with small hearts & leaves quilted in a circle, lace around each square. $405.00

7171288 – *BOTTOM RIGHT:* DOUBLE WEDDING RING; 90" x 102"; pastels on white; cotton; made in Illinois in 1988; machine pieced, hand quilted. $288.00

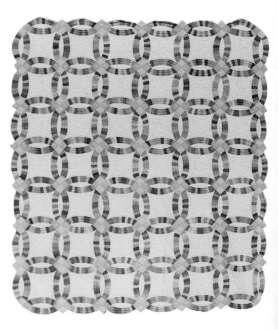

1181288 – *TOP LEFT:* HONEY BEE; 88" x 106"; brown & aqua on off-white; all cotton; made in 1980; machine pieced, hand quilted, hand appliqued. $414.00

2181288 – *TOP RIGHT:* 8 POINTED STAR; 68" x 68"; red, pink, green, blue, etc.; cottons; made in New England c. 1932; hand pieced, hand quilted; colorful & gay, perfect to brighten a young person's room; pink sateen backing. $432.00

3181288 – *CENTER LEFT:* GRANDMOTHER'S FAN; 103" x 103"; polyester & cotton print; muslin background & lining; hand quilted, machine pieced; multi-colored fans. $288.00

4181288 – *CENTER:* COUNTRY TULIP; 100" x 104"; mauve & green; 100% cotton percale; made in Kentucky in 1987; hand quilted, hand appli-

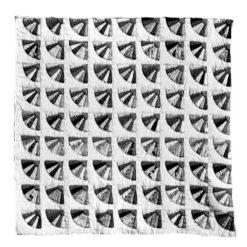

qued; 100% white percale, color fast appliques, Mountain Mist polyester filling. $575.00

5181288 – *CENTER RIGHT:* TREE OF LIFE; 86" x 100"; multi-color on white; cotton & cotton blend; made in Kentucky in 1988; hand quilted, hand appliqued. $345.00

6181288 – *BOTTOM LEFT:* CUBE ACCENT; 99" x 104"; blue; cotton/polyester; made in Missouri in 1988; hand pieced, hand quilted, machine pieced; 100% polyester batting. $405.00

7181288 – *BOTTOM RIGHT:* FLORAL CENTERPIECE; 88" x 102"; solid beige background, beige print basket & green flower; 100% cotton with bonded polyester batting; made in Missouri in 1985; hand pieced, hand quilted; basket block set on point with plain block set between; diamond zig-zag border; has won four blue ribbons in S.W. Missouri. $575.00

1191288 – *TOP LEFT:* U.S.A.; 96" x 113"; red, white & blue with cross stitching on blue & white gingham; poly blend checked blue gingham & solids; made in Texas in 1981; machine pieced, hand quilted; quilt was constructed by the women of Asbury United Methodist Church; dated & signed. $595.00

2191288 – *TOP RIGHT:* DRESDEN PLATE; 82" x 96"; pastel shades on ecru; cotton; made in Illinois in 1988; hand quilted, machine pieced. $265.00

3191288 – *CENTER LEFT:* MEMORIES IN PATCHWORK, Series Archway Pattern ©; 48" x 48"; silver gray print & white; poly/blend; made in Texas in 1988; machine pieced, hand quilted; designed for the names of the anniversary couple dates, with where they were married to be added using fabric paint as embroidery thread, white

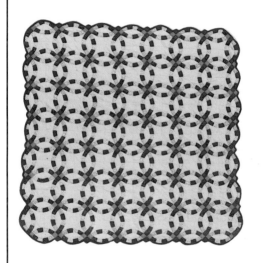

quilted hearts can have guests & family written on to form a lasting memory of a happy occasion. $115.00

4191288 – *CENTER:* LOG CABIN; 78" x 90"; yellows/natural muslin; cotton/cotton polyester; made in California in 1988; hand pieced, hand quilted; polyester batting, all new materials, flower print backing. $230.00

5191288 – *CENTER RIGHT:* DOUBLE WEDDING RING; 82½" x 83½"; multi-color; cotton & cotton blends; made in Tennessee in 1988; machine pieced, hand quilted; muslin background set together with red & gold; binding red. $375.00

6191288 – *BOTTOM LEFT:* FANCY FAN; 86" x 106"; muslin background, fan is print; polyester; machine pieced, hand quilted; made in 1980; $288.00

7191288 – *BOTTOM RIGHT:* SOLID UNBLEACHED; 99" x 127"; cotton/cotton poly blend; made in Illinois in 1988; machine pieced, hand quilted; unbleached muslin/peach reversible. $230.00

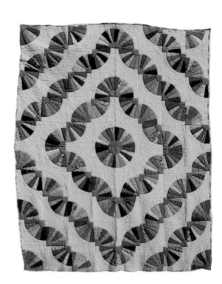

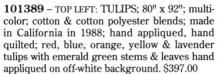

101389 – TOP LEFT: TULIPS; 80" x 92"; multi-color; cotton & cotton polyester blends; made in California in 1988; hand appliqued, hand quilted; red, blue, orange, yellow & lavender tulips with emerald green stems & leaves hand appliqued on off-white background. $397.00

201389 – TOP RIGHT: FLOWER BASKET, 84" x 84"; red, green & white; cotton; made in Pennsylvania in 1890's; hand pieced, hand quilted, hand appliqued; excellent condition $547.00

301389 – CENTER LEFT: ROSE GARDEN COLONIAL; 88" x 106"; cotton; hand quilted, hand appliqued. $460.00

401389 – CENTER: LOG CABIN: 73" x 88"; blues, mauves; cottons/polyester batting; made in Indiana in 1988; machine pieced, hand quilted; blocks are quilted into diamond pattern. $405.00

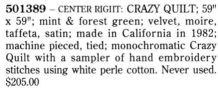

501389 – CENTER RIGHT: CRAZY QUILT; 59" x 59"; mint & forest green; velvet, moire, taffeta, satin; made in California in 1982; machine pieced, tied; monochromatic Crazy Quilt with a sampler of hand embroidery stitches using white perle cotton. Never used. $205.00

601389 – BOTTOM LEFT: DOUBLE IRISH CHAIN; 80" x 103"; light pink, dark coral, flowered print of browns, peach & greens; cottons; made in Missouri in 1987; machine pieced, hand quilted; polyester batting, backing calico print of pink/coral. $289.00

701389 – BOTTOM RIGHT: SAMPLER; 100" x 120"; light gold & rust; sashing is cotton, light gold is cotton/poly; made in Florida in 1985; machine pieced, hand quilted. $317.00

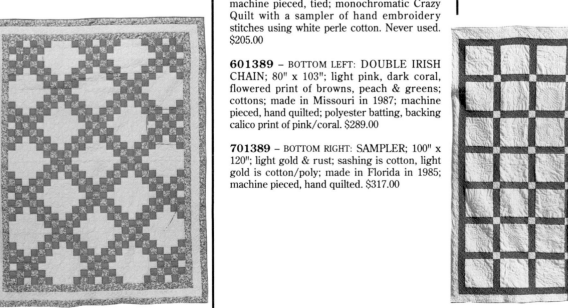

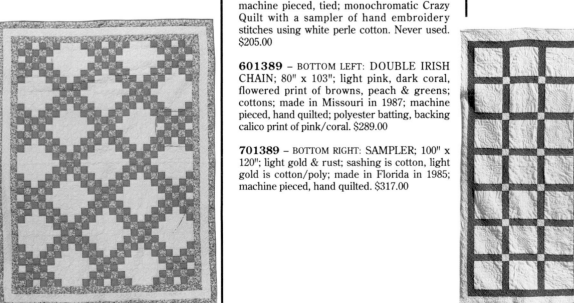

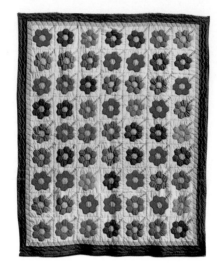

102389 – TOP LEFT: KALEIDOSCOPE; 70" x 80"; orchid pink with multi-color scraps; cottons with polyester batting; made in Indiana in 1987; machine pieced, hand quilted; backing is orchid pink. $317.00

202389 – TOP RIGHT: PANSY; 79" x 102"; multi with brown & yellow border; cotton; made in Indiana in 1980; hand pieced, hand quilted, hand appliqued; hand quilted by Amish. $288.00

302389 – CENTER LEFT: BABY BLOCKS; 72" x 82"; blue & white; cotton/poly; made in North Carolina in 1979; machine pieced, hand quilted. $259.00

402389 – CENTER: FLOWER TRAIL; 80" x 92"; rust, gold & white; cotton poly; made in Illinois in 1987; machine pieced, machine quilted; queen size, two hand embroidered blocks. $345.00

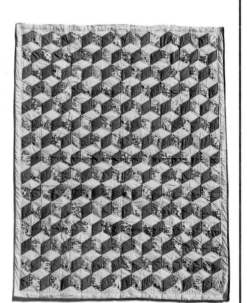

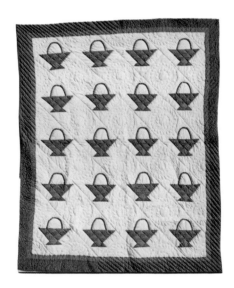

502389 – CENTER RIGHT: BASKET; 78" x 96"; blue & rose; cotton; made in Kentucky; hand quilted, hand appliqued. $345.00

602389 – BOTTOM LEFT: DRESDEN PLATE; 83" x 106"; green, peach, pink, clay colors; cottons; made in Missouri in 1986; machine pieced, hand quilted, hand appliqued; quilting motifs in fans, hearts, tulips with polyester batting, off-white on backing fabric. $432.00

702389 – BOTTOM RIGHT: PATCHWORK; 86" x 79"; variety of colors; cotton/polyester blends; made in Michigan in 1988; machine pieced; backed with a flannel sheet which has been preshrunk, quilt is tied with red embroidery floss. $276.00

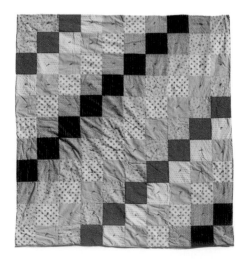

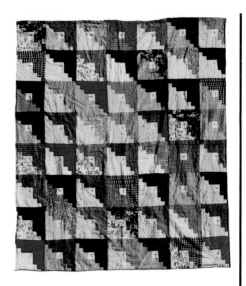

103389 – TOP LEFT: LOG CABIN; 79" x 92"; variety of colors; cotton-polyester; made in Michigan in 1988; machine pieced; backing is light blue flannel sheet which has been preshrunk; quilt is tied with red embroidery floss. $276.00

203389 – TOP RIGHT: STATE BIRDS; 82" x 95"; white with different color embroidery thread; cotton percale with muslin backing; made in Georgia in 1986; machine pieced, hand quilted, cross stitched; pre-stamped. $690.00

303389 – CENTER LEFT: "OLD MAID'S PUZZLE"; 94" x 94"; pink/brown/muslin; cotton; made in South Carolina c. 1860; hand pieced, hand quilted; fine quilting in feathered circles & pineapples, cabled borders, very few worn spots–one age stain along border. $460.00

403389 – CENTER: HEARTS & FLOWERS; 77½" x 90"; white percale & colored cotton; made in Georgia in 1988; machine pieced, hand quilted, hand appliqued; hearts & flowers

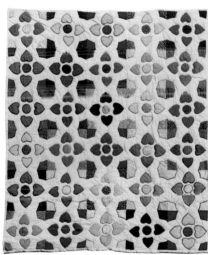

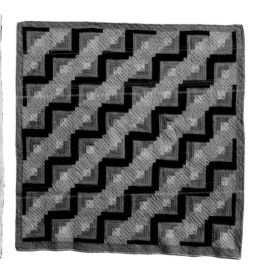

are made from solid & print cotton, polyester lining & percale backing. $460.00

503389 – CENTER RIGHT: LOG CABIN (straight furrows); 85" x 85"; blue & beige; 100% cotton, made in Maine in 1988; machine pieced, hand quilted; quilted diagonally on beige, around seams on blue, chain quilted on border, dark blue back with low-loft fiberfill, signed & dated on back in embroidery. $345.00

603389 – BOTTOM LEFT: DOUBLE WEDDING RING; 86" x 90"; pink/lavender prominent colors; cotton, cotton blends; made in Alabama in 1988; machine pieced, hand quilted; used baby prints with sheet lining & pink border with poly batting. $345.00

703389 – BOTTOM RIGHT: ATTIC WINDOW; 80" x 97"; red, white, aqua, basic colors with multi-colored fabric accents; made in Montana in 1986; machine pieced, hand quilted; very pretty & bright quilt with white backing. $403.00

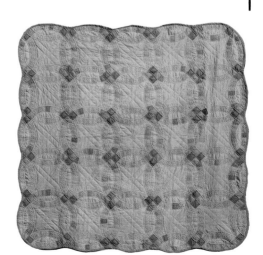

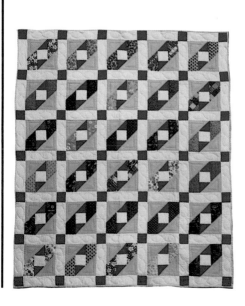

60

104389 – TOP LEFT: TRIP AROUND THE WORLD; 84" x 94"; pastel colors; cotton, cotton blends; made in Alabama in 1988; machine pieced, hand quilted; sheet lining with poly batting. $345.00.

204389 – TOP RIGHT: AUTUMN I LOVE YOU, Sampler Quilt; 75" x 92"; autumn in all its splendor; cottons, blends, rayons & challis; made in California in 1987; hand pieced, hand quilted; Fairfield traditional batting. $1,495.00

304389 – CENTER LEFT: LEAVES; 72" x 84"; white background, yellow sashing & multi-colored leaves; cotton; made in North Carolina in 1979; hand quilted, hand appliqued. $345.00

404389 – CENTER: DOUBLE WEDDING RING; 87" x 102"; multi-color with blue being

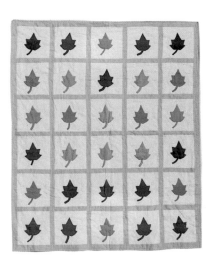

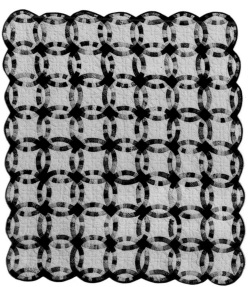

predominant; cotton & cotton blend; made in Kentucky. $345.00

504389 – CENTER RIGHT: FEATHER AND STAR; 90" x 104"; medium lavender & white; 100% cotton; made in Montana in 1987; hand quilted, hand appliqued; has scalloped edges, front & back lavender are the same fabric, can be used as a reversible quilt. $460.00

604389 – BOTTOM LEFT: DOUBLE IRISH CHAIN; 84" x 106"; blue & white; all cotton; made in Kentucky in 1988; machine pieced. $345.00

704389 – BOTTOM RIGHT: GRANDMOTHERS FAN; 89" x 89"; multi-pastels; cotton; made in Wisconsin in 1988; machine pieced, hand quilted. $690.00

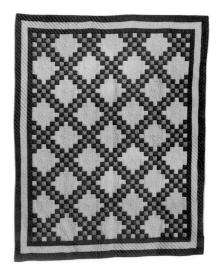

105389 – TOP LEFT: PLAIN, BLOCK; 72" x 89"; mixed colors; made in Delaware c. 1970; has been stored, never used. $145.00

205389 – TOP RIGHT: HEARTS DELIGHT; 86" x 106"; mauve, soft rose, touches of blue; made in Indiana in 1988; hand quilted, hand appliqued; hearts appliqued on blend, stripped with calico print with same binding on scalloped edge, border has no seams, backing parchment, 100% polyester fill. $575.00

305389 – CENTER LEFT: TRIP AROUND THE WORLD; 72" x 88"; variegated; polyester knits with 50/50 blend lining; made in Kentucky in 1987; hand pieced, machine pieced; very colorful & durable, completely washable, makes pretty wallhanging, reversible to show quilting pattern of rose & butterfly. $175.00

405389 – CENTER: LOG CABIN; 72" x 82"; blue; 50/50 cotton & poly blends; made in Kentucky in 1987; machine pieced, machine

quilted; can be used for tablecloth, completely washable (no chlorine), perfect for a country room decor. $259.00

505389 – CENTER RIGHT: LONE STAR; 93" x 98"; blue; cotton polyester; made in Missouri in 1988; machine pieced, hand quilted; 100% polyester fill. $345.00

605389 – BOTTOM LEFT: MIRROR IMAGE FAN; 86" x 96"; rainbow colors; cotton polyester; made in Missouri in 1988; machine pieced, hand quilted; the colors are blue, yellow, rose & peach, each fan the same, has cotton polyester fabric with polyester fill. $345.00

705389 – BOTTOM RIGHT: BETTY BOOP; 72" x 90"; cream & green; 50/50 poly & cotton blends; made in West Virginia in 1986; hand painted, machine pieced; machine washable (no bleach), polyester batting. $205.00

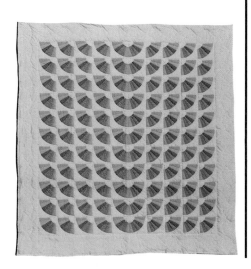

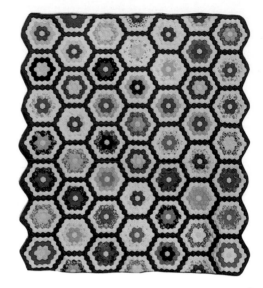

106389 – TOP LEFT: GRANDMOTHER'S FLOWER GARDEN; 100" x 112"; white & purple with variegated blocks; 50/50 poly & cotton blends; made in Kentucky in 1986; hand pieced, hand quilted; machine washable (no bleach). $345.00

206389 – TOP RIGHT: DOUBLE IRISH CHAIN; 95" x 106"; mauve/dusty pink; cotton/poly; made in Missouri in 1988; machine pieced, hand quilted; Dacron batting, made by Mennonite, off-white background, flower quilting design, signed & dated. $414.00

306389 – CENTER LEFT: DOUBLE WEDDING RING; 69" x 95"; dusty blue; cotton/poly; made in Missouri in 1988; machine pieced, hand quilted; made by Mennonites; off-white background. $289.00

406389 – CENTER: GODS EYE; 82" x 98"; browns & cream; cotton blends; made in

Pennsylvania in 1988; machine pieced, hand quilted; bound edge-brown print back. $289.00

506389 – CENTER RIGHT: STARLIGHT; 60" x 96"; green, brown & yellow; cotton blends; made in Pennsylvania in 1985; machine pieced, hand quilted; bound edge with solid yellow back. $202.00

606389 – BOTTOM LEFT: IRIS BLOSSOM; 77" x 100"; purple, lavender, orange, pastel print with white background; broadcloth & print polyester filling with white sheet lining; made in Tennessee in 1988; hand pieced, hand quilted; design circa 1930's. $345.00

706389 – BOTTOM RIGHT: PANSY; 102" x 102"; lavender on white; cotton; made in Illinois in 1986; hand pieced, hand quilted; appliqued pansy on white with embroidery thread, set together with light lavender. $276.00

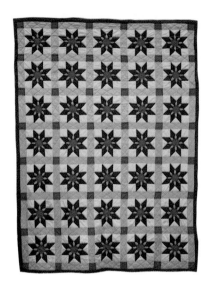

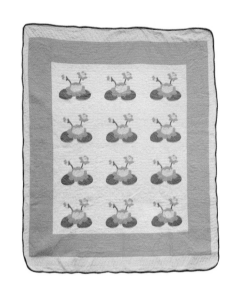

107389 – TOP LEFT: "MISSOURI DAISY"; 80" x 104"; apricots & coordinating shades of brown solids & prints; 100% cotton with polyester batting; made in Kansas in 1986; hand pieced, hand quilted; signed & dated. $230.00

207389 – TOP RIGHT: WATERLILY; 75" x 95"; yellow, green & white; cotton; made in Pennsylvania in 1930; hand quilted, hand appliqued. $363.00

307389 – CENTER LEFT: CONFLICTING PERSPECTIVES; 90" x 100" black, light pink & blue, hot pink & blue; muslin, cotton blends, upholstery fabrics; made in Connecticut in 1977; machine pieced, hand quilted; bold graphic design intended for wallhanging. $173.00

407389 – CENTER: DOUBLE IRISH CHAIN VARIATION; 66" x 82"; dark green, oxblood, rose check; cotton; made in Pennsylvania in 1900; hand pieced, hand quilted. $420.00

507389 – CENTER RIGHT: STATES; 98" x 104"; white with blue lettering; cotton; made in Illinois in 1985; hand pieced, hand quilted; embroidery birds & flowers of 50 states, lettering in blue, set together with blocks of stars on white. $299.00

607389 – BOTTOM LEFT: PYRAMID; 76½" x 106"; multi-colored print; cotton & cotton blends; made in Arkansas in 1988; hand quilted, machine pieced; muslin backing, polyester batting a dark rose, border with multi-colored prints, quilted around each seam. $230.00

707389 – BOTTOM RIGHT: OFF-CENTERED LOG CABIN; 96" x 106"; shades of dark & light blues; poly cotton blends with many VIP prints; made in Illinois in 1988; machine pieced, machine quilted; different variation of Log Cabin block, bonded poly batting, binding is double fabric & double stitched, has blue lining. $259.00

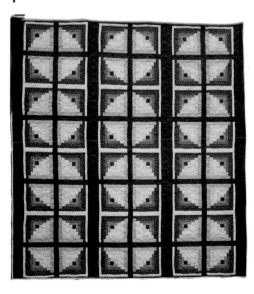

108389 – TOP LEFT: DOUBLE IRISH CHAIN; 90" x 108"; mint green, ruby; unbleached muslin, poly/cotton blends; made in Connecticut in 1980; machine pieced, hand quilted; traditional design with feather circle & double cable quilting patterns, a multi-award winner. $575.00

208389 – TOF RIGHT: LOG CABIN; 84" x 110"; navy blue centers & multi-colored; cotton/polyester; made in Missouri in 1988; machine pieced, hand quilted; polyester batting. $345.00

308389 – CENTER LEFT: STRING-PIECED STAR; 70" x 98"; multi-colors; cotton fabrics & batting; made in Kansas in 1930's; hand pieced, hand quilted; never used, never washed, fabrics span many years, many different fabrics, dress pieces, flour-sack fabrics, etc. $403.00

408389 – CENTER: CHAIN LINK; 87" x 106"; blues; poly cotton blends; made in Illinois in 1988; machine pieced, machine quilted; old

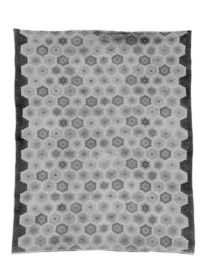

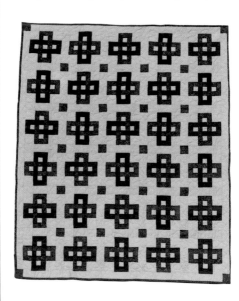

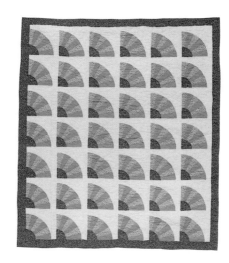

pattern made in blues with a bonded poly batting, binding is double fabric & double stitched. $202.00

508389 – CENTER RIGHT: GRANDMOTHER'S FAN; 72" x 84"; winter print with rose & small print; cotton & polyester; made in 1988; machine quilted, hand appliqued; new material, polyester batting, heading & name on back, never been used. $145.00

608389 – BOTTOM LEFT: GRANDMOTHER'S BABY FLOWER GARDEN; 63½" x 79"; very light pastels; cotton; made in Kentucky in 1925; hand pieced, hand quilted; has light pastels, pinks, blues, browns & assorted prints, pieces are much smaller than traditional Flower Garden. $345.00

708389 – BOTTOM RIGHT: GRANDMOTHER'S FAN; 79" x 98"; solid mauve & print mixed; broadcloth, made in Kentucky in 1985; hand pieced, hand quilted. $175.00

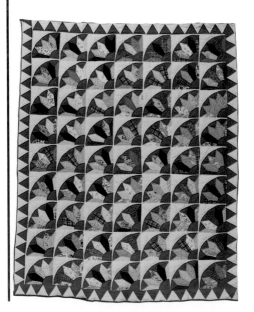

109389 – TOP LEFT: "CRAZY" SCRAP QUILT; 67" x 86"; multi-color; cotton; made in Tennessee in 1940; hand pieced, hand quilted; has blue backing. $230.00

209389 – TOP RIGHT: FRILLED DUTCH DOLL; 82" x 100"; navy blue; cotton; made in 1988; hand pieced, hand quilted; pattern taken from a 1952 flour sack, navy blue with red hearts & muslin background, not much quilting but very unique. $386.00

309389 – CENTER LEFT: 9 PATCH VARIATION; 69" x 77½"; mixed, cotton; made in Tennessee in 1940; hand pieced, hand quilted; mixture of prints with lots of different blues & set together with blue calico. $288.00

409389 – CENTER: CATHEDRAL WINDOW; 63" x 80"; multi-colors; muslin backing with cottons & blends; made in Maine in 1982; hand

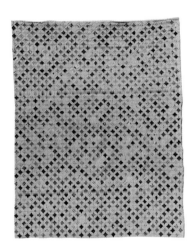

pieced, hand appliqued; all fabrics prewashed, signed & dated, contains 1,182 "windows". $489.00

509389 – CENTER RIGHT: SUNBONNET GIRL; 76" x 93"; rose with small red print; new cotton & polyester; made in Indiana in 1988; machine quilted, hand appliqued; polyester batting, heading & name on back, never been used. $145.00

609389 – BOTTOM LEFT: MONKEY WRENCH; 80" x 93"; solid rose pink, filling white with rose flowers; made in Arkansas in 1984; machine pieced, hand quilted; backing is light rose, polyester batting. $230.00

709389 – BOTTOM RIGHT: EIGHT POINT STAR; 72" x 91"; solid mixed colors; cotton blends; made in Ohio in 1980; hand pieced, hand quilted. $175.00

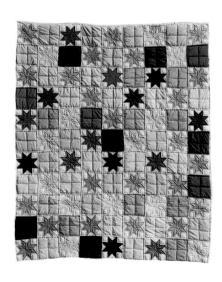

66

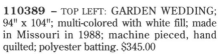

110389 – TOP LEFT: GARDEN WEDDING; 94" x 104"; multi-colored with white fill; made in Missouri in 1988; machine pieced, hand quilted; polyester batting. $345.00

210389 – TOP RIGHT: GREEN BRICK WALK; 80" x 88"; green; made in Indiana in 1930's; hand quilted; made as a pair with pink brick walk. $317.00

310389 – CENTER LEFT: STAR TYPE; 72" x 76½"; orange/black/pink/blue/grey/brown; cotton; made in Kentucky in 1945; hand pieced, hand quilted; diamond-shaped star with bold orange black set together with tan & brown, backing quilted in fans. $230.00

410389 – CENTER: PINK STARS; 58" x 75"; made in Indiana in 1870's; hand pieced, hand quilted. $405.00

510389 – CENTER RIGHT: PRINCESS FEATHER; 78" x 78"; red/yellow/green with muslin; cotton & cotton/poly 50/50, batting is Dacron polyfil, back is 50/50 & binding is cotton; made in Arkansas in 1988; hand pieced, hand quilted, hand appliqued; unlike other traditional Princess Feather with all solids, the red in this one is a print with bits of the yellow & green in it, quilted in thread to match so the back shows red/green & yellow as well as neutral thread. $289.00

610389 – BOTTOM LEFT: PIECED ROSE; 82" x 92"; yellow & green on white; broadcloth, polyester filling, bleached sheet lining; made in Tennessee in 1987; hand pieced, hand quilted; 1930 pattern. $345.00

710389 – BOTTOM RIGHT: "FEED SACKS"; 67" x 87" ; pink, green, lavender; cotton; made in Arkansas in 1940's; machine pieced, hand quilted; hand-dyed feed sacks, some printing visible, muslin backing. $173.00

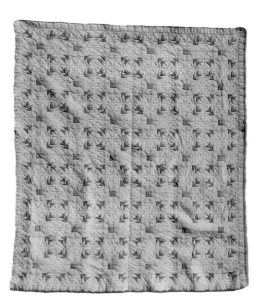

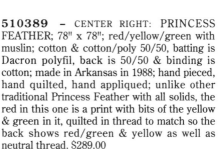

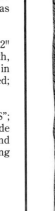

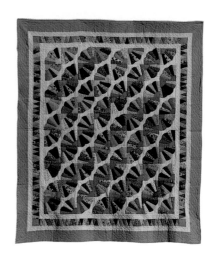

111389 – TOP LEFT: ROYAL STAR OF MISSISSIPPI; 89" x 95"; rust & brown; cotton/polyester; made in Missouri in 1988; machine pieced, hand quilted; prints & solids, cream fill & backing polyester-cotton with polyester batting. $345.00

211389 – TOP RIGHT: FANS; 85" x 103"; multi-colored prints & aqua; cotton prints & backgrounds; made in Illinois in 1985; machine pieced, hand quilted; set together to suggest movement, border is made of triangles of same prints. $375.00

311389 – CENTER LEFT: HEARTS IN THE PINK; 82" x 91"; pink & cream; cotton prints & plain; made in Illinois in 1988; machine pieced, hand quilted, hand appliqued; hearts are backed with polyester batting so each is puffed & quilted. $345.00

411389 – CENTER: PEACHES AND CREAM; 89" x 104"; shades of peaches & creams; 100% cottons; made in Virginia in 1987; machine pieced, hand quilted, hand appliqued;

Grandmother's Fan pattern, diagonal setting, solid cream back, abundant hand quilting, tiny stitches shows beautifully on both sides, double fabric binding, signed & dated. $575.00

511389 – CENTER RIGHT: ROYAL STAR OF WEST VIRGINIA; 88" x 91"; blues; polyester-cotton; made in Missouri in 1988; machine pieced, hand quilted; solids & prints, polyester-cotton, white fill & backing, polyester batting. $345.00

611389 – BOTTOM LEFT: 8 POINT STAR; 70" x 79½"; multi-color; cotton; made in Tennessee in 1940; hand pieced, hand quilted; assorted prints & solids set together with pink & tan, quilted in fans, lightweight. $345.00

711389 – BOTTOM RIGHT: LOG CABIN (Courthouse Steps); 68" x 73"; red/black/blue/orange; cotton; made in Tennessee in 1935; hand pieced, hand quilted; has black center with red, blue, orange, pink all blending in., has a rustic appeal accented with bold type colors. $156.00

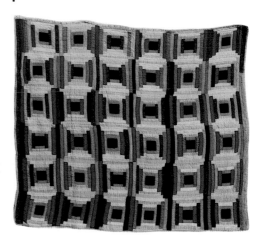

68

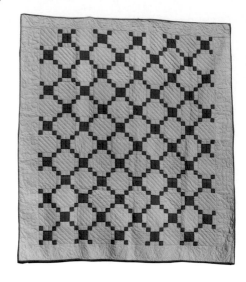

112389 – TOP LEFT: IRISH CHAIN; 98" x 110"; light & dark blue; polyester-cotton; made in Illinois in 1987; machine pieced, hand quilted; reversible, quilted with dark blue quilting thread, light blue lining. $230.00

212389 – TOP RIGHT: STELLA'S STRING QUILT; 73" x 89"; predominantly navy, yellow & brown; cotton & cotton blends; made in Arkansas in 1950's; hand pieced, machine pieced, hand quilted; muslin backing, very colorful, quilted border. $230.00

312389 – CENTER LEFT: 8 POINT STRING STAR; 69½" x 79½"; pinks/blues predominant; cotton; made in Tennessee in 1930; hand pieced, hand quilted; old-fashioned string star quilt, very colorful, does have minor rips. $345.00

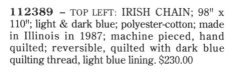

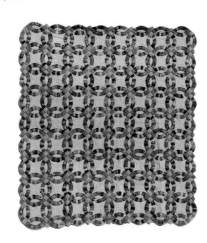

412389 – CENTER: DOUBLE WEDDING RING; 73" x 84"; multi-color; cotton; made in Tennessee in 1948; hand pieced, hand quilted; set together with green & yellow squares, scalloped edges, lightweight. $345.00

512389 – CENTER RIGHT: MAGENTA BRICK WALK; 80" x 95"; made in Indiana in 1930's; hand quilted. $317.00

612389 – BOTTOM LEFT: SQUARES WITHIN A SQUARE; 78½" x 89½"; mixed prints & solids; cotton & cotton blends; made in Tennessee in 1945; hand pieced, hand quilted; set together with yellow & black strips. $205.00

712389 – BOTTOM RIGHT: RAIL FENCE; 96" x 107"; brown, yellow & pattern rose prints; polyester cotton; made in Illinois in 1988; machine pieced, hand quilted; reversible, quilted in brown thread. $230.00

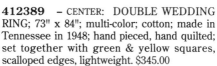

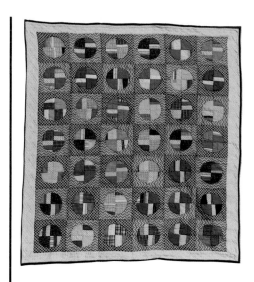

113389 – TOP LEFT: "GRANDMOTHER'S FLOWER GARDEN"; 70" x 78"; multi-prints & solids; made in Pennsylvania c. 1935; hand quilted. $259.00

213389 – TOP RIGHT: STRIPPY QUILT; 82" x 94"; multi-muslin but predominantly blue/green; cotton top, dacron polyfil batting, 50/50 backing muslin, cotton binding; made in Arkansas in 1987; hand pieced, hand quilted; scrap quilt. $202.00

313389 – CENTER LEFT: TRIP AROUND THE WORLD; 71½" x 78"; mixed; cotton; made in Tennessee in 1945; hand pieced, hand quilted; very colorful with solids & mixed prints, 1½" blocks. $405.00

413389 – CENTER: "DOVE AT THE WINDOW"; 70" x 81"; red/orange/white; cottons; border is machine appliqued, hand quilted; made c. 1900; small tear in one of the corner "doves", otherwise excellent. $489.00

513389 – CENTER RIGHT: "GRANDMOTHER'S FLOWER GARDEN"; 62½" x 79½"; multi-color; cotton; made in Tennessee in 1945; hand pieced, hand quilted; muslin backing, lightweight. $357.00

613389 – BOTTOM LEFT: LAVENDER SAWTOOTH DIAMOND; 62" x 81"; lavender; made in 1920-40; machine pieced, hand appliqued. $405.00

713389 – BOTTOM RIGHT: BARS AND NINE PATCH; 30" x 38"; blue & white; 100% cotton; made in Wisconsin in 1988; machine pieced, hand quilted. $58.00

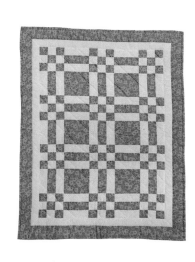

114389 – TOP LEFT: CASTLE WALL W/KALEIDOSCOPE CENTERS; 46" x 66"; dusty blues & dusty pink w/turquoise accent; all cottons/Jinny Beyer's RJR stripe; made in Florida in 1988; machine pieced, hand quilted; original designs, signed & dated, sleeve for hanging, Mountain Mist polyester batting. $460.00

214389 – TOP RIGHT: TREASURE QUEST; 42" x 42"; purple, grey, black; cotton; made in Pennsylvania in 1987; machine pieced, hand quilted; features sharp, geometric design, no markings on quilt, hanging sleeve has been permanently applied. $145.00

314389 – CENTER LEFT: UNDER MOTHER'S WING; 44" x 58"; light aqua solid, aqua, pink & yellow print; cotton; made in 1988; machine pieced, hand appliqued, hand quilted, center is also hand tied; Mother Goose & 3 goslings, there is a stuffed gosling in Mother's wing which is a removable toy, center is solid aqua with a print border & a pink heart in each corner. $115.00

414389 – CENTER: "BABY BLUES"; 42" x 56½"; baby blue with coordinated blue cotton;

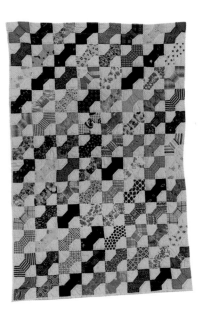

100% cotton; made in New Jersey in 1980; hand quilted; whole cloth design, can be used for young child's bed or wallhanging. $60.00

514389 – CENTER RIGHT: NECKTIE; 37" x 60"; white & multi-color, backing is white; mostly cotton, few poly-cotton pieces; made in Kansas in 1987; machine pieced, hand quilted; blocks pieced in 1950's, never used, most blocks are different, some fabrics appear older than 1950's, backing fabric brought to front for a binding. $87.00

614389 – BOTTOM LEFT: HEARTS AROUND; 30" x 30"; pinks & soft greens; 100% cotton; made in Colorado in 1987; hand quilted, hand appliqued; appliqued hearts are surrounded by quilted border of intertwined hearts, quilted in pink thread. $87.00

714389 – BOTTOM RIGHT: LOG CABIN – BARN RAISING; 42" x 42"; browns, rusts, beige's with traditional red "chimneys"; 100% (prewashed) cotton; made in North Carolina in 1988; handsome "scrap look," each "log" quilted down center, border in cable design, sleeve for hanging, signed & dated. $138.00

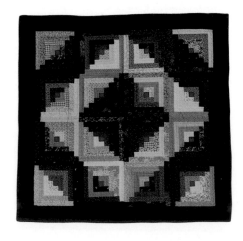

115389 – TOP LEFT: LOG CABIN; 50" x 50"; multi-color with medium purple; cotton/-polyester; made in Missouri in 1987; machine pieced, hand quilted; polyester batting. $75.00

215389 – TOP RIGHT: PAINTED QUILT; 44" x 44"; cream background with orange border; cotton/polyester; made in Missouri in 1988; machine pieced, hand quilted; polyester batting, quilted around painted pictures. $75.00

315389 – CENTER LEFT: "FAN" or "WHEEL"; 75" x 78"; mixed colors with rose/pink background; mostly cotton, made c. 1974; hand pieced, hand quilted; pieced at least 15 years ago, it is Fan pattern but was put together to resemble a wheel. $200.00

415389 – CENTER: TRIP AROUND THE WORLD (Variation); 82½" x 110"; pastels; all 100% cotton; made in Florida in 1988; machine

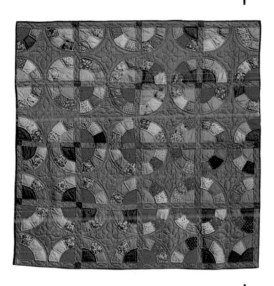

pieced, hand quilted; polyester batting, backing is off-white, muslin, materials were pre-washed before being cut. $345.00

515389 – CENTER RIGHT: MISSOURI STAR; 67" x 96"; white blocks, brown, yellow lining, rust; broadcloth; machine pieced, hand quilted. $200.00

615389 – BOTTOM LEFT: GARDEN OF TULIPS & BUTTERFLY; 81" x 103"; rice, roses, mauves, Chinese blue, black & wine; 100% cotton; hand appliqued, hand quilted; quilted in feathers, flowers, vines & heart-shaped leaves. $430.00

715389 – BOTTOM RIGHT: 8 POINT STAR; 44" x 44"; burgundy & blue; cotton blends; made in Kentucky in 1989; machine pieced, hand quilted; polyester batting. $189.00

116389 – TOP LEFT: LONE STAR; 40½" x 40½"; multi-colored with black; cotton & polyester; made in Minnesota in 1985; hand pieced, hand quilted; several bright prints set against black background, has sleeve on back for hanging. $133.00

216389 – TOP RIGHT: AROUND THE WORLD; 36" x 36"; peach & brown; cotton & polyester; made in Minnesota in 1983; hand pieced, hand quilted; Drunkard's Path pattern in Around The World setting, sleeve on back for hanging. $105.00

316389 – CENTER LEFT: ROSE OF SHARON; 24" x 24"; soft greens, rose & gold; 100% cotton; made in Wisconsin in 1988; hand quilted, hand appliqued; Nancy Pearson-type applique using large prints & placing templates on chosen areas of design, poly batting. $87.00

416389 – CENTER: 6 POINT STRING STAR; 28" x 32"; mauve, grey, blue, clay; 100% cotton;

made in Indiana; solid colors, wallhanging. $145.00

516389 – CENTER RIGHT: ANIMAL CRIB QUILT; 46" x 56"; pink & white with pink, blue & yellow prints; cotton/poly; made in Illinois in 1987; machine pieced, machine quilted, hand embroidered; 12 animal blocks. $60.00

616389 – BOTTOM LEFT: MODIFIED RAIL FENCE; 32" x 32"; rusts & blues; cotton blends; made in Indiana in 1987; machine pieced, hand quilted; coordinating print back. $60.00

716389 – BOTTOM RIGHT: EVENING STAR; 36" x 48"; blues & pinks; 100% cotton; made in Maine in 1985; machine pieced, hand quilted; crib, wall or lap size, background is solid medium blue with assorted prints for star designs. $175.00

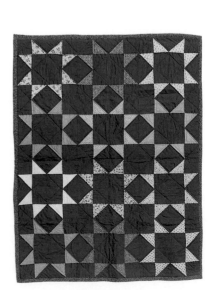

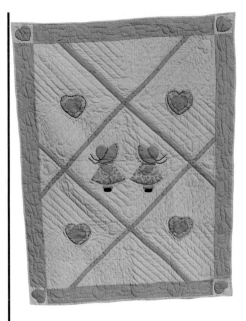

117389 – TOP LEFT: STRIP QUILTED LAP QUILT; 47" x 62½"; bright crayon colors; 100% cotton; made in Maine in 1986; machine pieced, hand quilted, machine quilted; child, lap or wall quilt, sewn in strips using a lot of bright, happy colors, for child's room or wallhanging, heart designs in corner blocks. $205.00

217389 – TOP RIGHT: SUNBONNET BABY; 42" x 55"; pink & white; broadcloth print, 63% polyester & 35% cotton; made in Indiana in 1987; hand quilted, hand appliqued; lace around bonnets, skirts & hearts, backing one piece, same material as front, 100% polyester fill. $115.00

317389 – CENTER LEFT: CHURN DASH; 42" x 55"; muslin & red; 100% cottons; made in Colorado in 1988; machine pieced, hand quilted; blocks set off by a sawtooth border, prairie point edging & swirling quilting lines, material was pre-washed. $161.00

417389 – CENTER: THE MIDNIGHT SEA; 33½" x 33½"; black/turquoise; satins, silks,

rayons, cottons, blends, hand silk screened cotton; made in California in 1984; hand & machine pieced, hand quilted; cathedral window to catch patches of light on the sea, inserts are strip pieced, embroidered, cotton outing flannel batting. $374.00

517389 – CENTER RIGHT: MEDICINE MAN; 36" x 36"; light blue, creme, turquoise, dark brown & red; 100% cottons; machine pieced, hand quilted; made in Virginia in 1988; heavily quilted on thin poly batting, double bias binding, signed & dated. $81.00

617389 – BOTTOM LEFT: BEAR QUILT; 44" x 44"; multi-color & light green; cotton/-polyester; made in Missouri in 1988; machine pieced, hand quilted, hand painted; polyester fill. $55.00

717389 – BOTTOM RIGHT: BEAR QUILT; 44" x 44"; multi-color & light green; cotton/-polyester; made in Missouri in 1988; machine pieced, hand quilted, hand painted; polyester fill. $55.00

74

118389 – TOP LEFT: BOY BUNNY; 38" x 44"; blue & white; cotton & blends; made in North Carolina in 1985; machine pieced, hand & machine quilted, machine appliqued; bunny dressed in overalls, shirt & cap with blue background surrounded by white & blue print squares, bunny is hand quilted. $70.00

218389 – TOP RIGHT: GIRL BUNNY; 38" x 44"; white, pink & green print; cotton & blends; made in North Carolina in 1985; machine pieced, hand & machine quilted, machine appliqued; bunny dressed in dress & pinafore with pink background surrounded by white, green & pink print squares, bunny is hand quilted. $70.00

318389 – CENTER LEFT: "PUA KALIKIMAKA," CHRISTMAS FLOWER; 42" x 52"; natural background with kelly border & central medallion, red blossoms; Imperial broadcloth with calico backing; made in Marshall Islands in 1987; hand quilted, hand appliqued; original design done in the Hawaiian quilting manner, lap quilt or wallhanging, machine wash & dry. $472.00

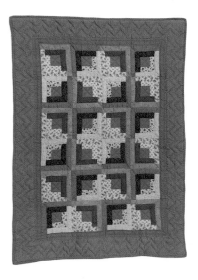

418289 – CENTER: OLA'S BEAUTY; 36" x 36"; Red Baron applique & border on dusty rose background, dusty rose quilt backing; Imperial Broadcloth; made in Marshall Islands in 1988; hand quilted, hand appliqued; wallhanging based on original design by Deborah U. Kakalia of Honolulu, Hawaii, echo quilting surrounding central applique, machine wash & dry. $167.00

518389 – CENTER RIGHT: LOG CABIN CRIB; 33" x 46"; pink/rose; cotton/poly; made in Illinois in 1988; machine pieced, hand quilted. $60.00

618389 – BOTTOM LEFT: BASKET WALLHANGING; 28" x 28"; brown, rust & beige; cotton/poly; made in Illinois in 1987; machine pieced, hand quilted. $65.00

718389 – BOTTOM RIGHT: DOUBLE IRISH CHAIN; 80" x 90"; green & white with white lining; cotton blend; made in Missouri in 1986; hand pieced, hand quilted; polyester batting, pre-washed, blue ribbon winner at County Fair, never been used. $345.00

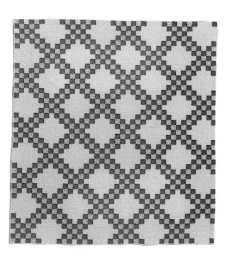

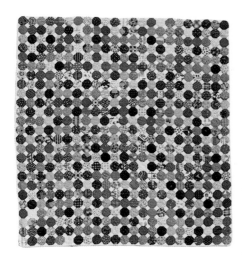

119389 – TOP LEFT: COBBLESTONES; 82" x 90"; multi-color prints on muslin background; cotton; made in Kentucky in 1987; hand pieced, hand quilted; polyester batting, light blue backing. $460.00

219389 – TOP RIGHT: DRESDEN PLATE; 84" x 112" (not including scalloped border); earth tones; made in Alabama; machine pieced, hand quilted; king-size quilt with scalloped border, quilt is even – photo isn't. $489.00

319389 – CENTER LEFT: "FOLK ART"; 70" x 72" (does not include lace measurement); red on white; cotton; made in Pennsylvania in 1910; hand embroidered, hand crochet 8" edge in addition to quilt itself, hand quilted; turkey red motifs on white. $328.00

419389 – CENTER: CHURN DASH; 76" x 92"; multi-color; cotton; made in Pennsylvania in

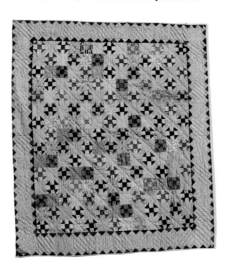

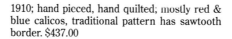

1910; hand pieced, hand quilted; mostly red & blue calicos, traditional pattern has sawtooth border. $437.00

519389 – CENTER RIGHT: LONE STAR; 88" x 88"; light pink to rose; polyester cotton; made in Tennessee in 1981; machine pieced, hand quilted. $230.00

619389 – BOTTOM LEFT: LONE STAR; 96" x 96"; earth tones; made in Tennessee; polyester & cotton print & solid with muslin lining; machine pieced, hand quilted. $259.00

719389 – BOTTOM RIGHT: DOUBLE WEDDING RING; 73" x 73"; cotton & polyester; made in Kentucky in 1987; hand & machine pieced, hand quilted; color-fast material, Mountain Mist batting, poly. $288.00

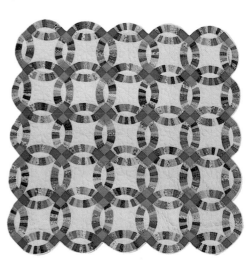

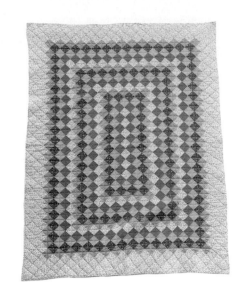

101689 – TOP LEFT: LITTLE BEECH TREE; 89" x 102"; shades of blue, green, rust, gold, red & tan with deep brown trunks on an off-white background; cotton & cotton blends; made in Louisiana in 1989; machine pieced, hand appliqued, hand quilted; colorful beech trees make a glorious setting on an off-white background that will enhance any decor. $805.00

201689 – TOP RIGHT: TRIP AROUND THE WORLD; 65" x 84"; cream, blues, mauves, pink; 100% cottons; made in Pennsylvania in 1988; machine pieced, hand quilted; unused, small stitches, 100% boned polyester batting. $259.00

301689 – CENTER LEFT: LEAVES; 80" x 100"; white background, appliqued pastel leaves, green borders & circles; scrap calico purchased in late 1920's & early 1930's; made in Wisconsin in 1936; heavily quilted, some greens are very faded. $345.00

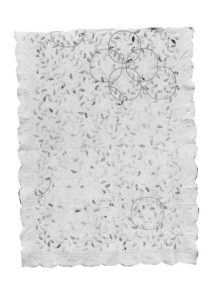

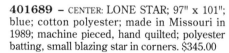

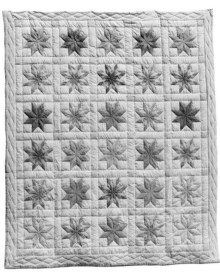

401689 – CENTER: LONE STAR; 97" x 101"; blue; cotton polyester; made in Missouri in 1989; machine pieced, hand quilted; polyester batting, small blazing star in corners. $345.00

501689 – CENTER RIGHT: BLAZING STAR; 85" x 100"; blue, green, peach & yellow; cotton/polyester; made in Missouri in 1989; machine pieced, hand quilted; multi-color, no block alike, polyester batting. $345.00.

601689 – BOTTOM LEFT: EVENING STAR; 80" x 96"; light green, dark green with floral stripe print & bright yellow; cotton; made in Montana & South Dakota in 1987; machine pieced, hand quilted; white cotton backing with dark green binding, very bright & colorful, polyester batting. $374.00.

701689 – BOTTOM RIGHT: RAINBOW AROUND THE WORLD; 71" x 85"; dark purple; cotton; made in New Mexico in 1988; machine pieced, machine quilted; filling is Orlon Dacron piling. $230.00

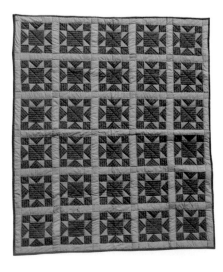

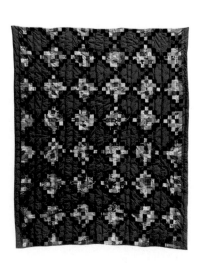

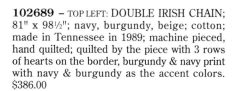

102689 – TOP LEFT: DOUBLE IRISH CHAIN; 81" x 98½"; navy, burgundy, beige; cotton; made in Tennessee in 1989; machine pieced, hand quilted; quilted by the piece with 3 rows of hearts on the border, burgundy & navy print with navy & burgundy as the accent colors. $386.00

202689 – TOP RIGHT: STARBURST; 84" x 99"; shades of brown calico prints, plain brown & cream accents; cotton; made in Montana & South Dakota in 1988; machine pieced & hand quilted; polyester batting, fine quilting stitches, fits queen bed, backing is cream cotton which matches the front accent & has brown binding. $460.00

302689 – CENTER LEFT: STEPPING STONES; 62" x 80"; blue, rose & green; 100% cotton; machine pieced, hand tied; double batt (Mountain Mist) with blue flannel sheet blanket on back, never used. $202.00

402689 – CENTER: SISTER'S CHOICE; 78" x 96"; blue print with rose & beige solid; polyester blends & cotton; made in Arkansas in 1987; machine pieced, hand quilted; quilted

around each seam, poly batting, muslin backing bound in rose, binding is double. $230.00

502689 – CENTER RIGHT: TWELVE TRIANGLES; 80" x 92"; multi-colored with cream background; cottons/cotton blends with cotton backing; made in Virginia in 1989; machine pieced, hand quilted; bonded Lowloft polyester batting. $368.00

602689 – BOTTOM LEFT: WHEEL OF FORTUNE; 82" x 90"; aqua & gold; cotton & cotton/polyester; made in Wisconsin in 1976; machine pieced, hand quilted; aqua, gold & mixed prints on muslin background, black & gold border; gold backing, cotton filler, fabric pre-washed. $432.00

702689 – BOTTOM RIGHT: GRANDMOTHER'S FAN; 72" x 84"; yellow; cotton & polyester blends; made in Arkansas in 1983; machine pieced, hand quilted; fans are print & solid, the blocks are filled out with yellow, white sheet polyester blend for backing, polyester batting double binding in white quilted around most seams. $230.00

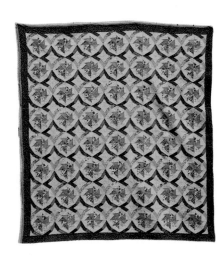

103689 – TOP LEFT: CHEERS TO THE RED, WHITE AND BLUE!; 77" x 92"; red, white & blue; cotton; made in Illinois in 1977; hand pieced, hand quilted; made as a quilted "Hurrah!" to America's bicentennial celebration, Up-beat Americana mood. $460.00

203689 – TOP RIGHT: COUNTRY SUNRISE; 89" x 102"; shades of rose & blue; cotton-poly; made in Oregon in 1988; machine pieced, hand quilted; Log Cabin piecing method used to create a medallion quilt in popular country colors. $288.00

303689 – CENTER LEFT: BEAR'S PAWS; 75" x 93"; colonial green & peach; cotton/poly print & solids; made in Virginia in 1989; machine piece, hand quilted; pastel interpretation of an old traditional pattern, bonded poly batting, matching shade of a coordinating green print on backing, double bias edging, mitered corners, dated. $345.00

403689 – CENTER: BOW TIE QUILT; 63" x 81"; multi-color prints; 100% cotton; made in Indiana in 1989; machine pieced, hand quilted;

used multi-shades of muslin for "old-fashion quilt" look, backing is cotton-poly blend, signed & dated. $259.00

503689 – CENTER RIGHT: DRESDEN PLATE; 67" x 85"; gold cotton lining set together with pink strips; cotton; made in New Mexico in 1988; machine pieced, hand appliqued, hand quilted; polyester fill. $230.00

603689 – BOTTOM LEFT: "EARTH WREATH" (adapted from Aunt Sukey's Choice Block); 84" x 84"; brown, rusts & greens; 100% cottons/poly cottons; made in Arizona in 1986; machine pieced, hand quilted, embroidered with knots; inspired by large border print & is enhanced with French knots, never used, batting is Cotton Classic™. $862.00

703789 – BOTTOM RIGHT: GREEK CROSS SAMPLER; 94" x 94"; earth tones, (off-white, browns, tangarine); made in New Mexico in 1987; machine pieced, hand quilted; original design using sample blocks, 3rd place ribbon at 1987 New Mexico State Fair, never been used. $575.00

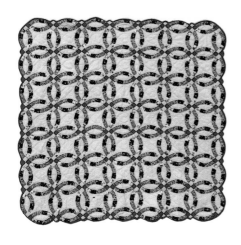

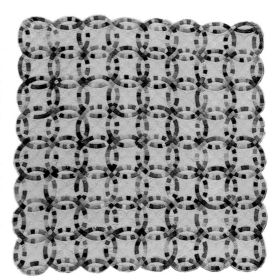

104689 – TOP LEFT: DOUBLE WEDDING RING; 81" x 84"; multi-color; cotton; made in Tennessee in 1989; machine pieced, hand quilted; has 4 different colors of roses, rose material is 100% cotton, muslin backing, quilted in hearts & by the piece. $374.00

204689 – TOP RIGHT: DOUBLE WEDDING RING; 100" x 100"; multi-color with cream background; cotton/polyester; made in Missouri in 1988; machine pieced, hand quilted; polyester fill. $345.00

304689 – CENTER LEFT: SQUARE WITHIN A SQUARE; 63" x 87"; red border with assorted colors; cotton & cotton feedsacks; made in Arkansas in 1940's; hand & machine pieced, hand quilted; colorful scrap quilt, prints & solids with red border. $230.00

404689 – CENTER: LANCASTER; 98" x 102"; rust; percale; cross stitched; stamped on eggshell percale & stitched by hand in rust

colors, Pennsylvania Dutch designs make this a popular quilt. $460.00

504689 – CENTER RIGHT: SAM AND SUE; 67" x 98"; blue; cotton/polyester; made in Missouri in 1988; machine pieced, hand quilted; multi-color on blue. $288.00

604689 – BOTTOM LEFT: STAINED GLASS; 95" x 107"; shades of greens, teal with black accent; cotton-poly mix; made in Oregon in 1987; machine pieced, hand quilted; postage stamp multi-color, tiny squares framed in black for medallion blocks, then framed in green to teal strips to set the medallions. $345.00

704689 – BOTTOM RIGHT: BOW TIE; 86" x 95"; predominately blue with pink & orchard; cotton/polyester blend; made in Ohio in 1986; machine pieced, hand quilted; pink & orchard calico bow ties separated with blue squares quilted in Dresden Plate design, quilted in off-white thread, blue backing, polyester batting. $345.00

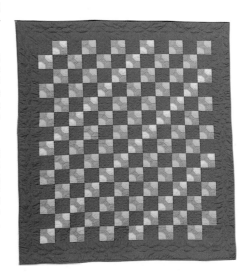

105689 – TOP LEFT: BAYOU SHOO-FLY & BUTTERFLIES; 82" x 94"; mauve, pink, blue & white; 100% cottons & poly-cottons; made in Louisiana in 1988; machine pieced, hand quilted, hand appliqued; pre-washed, poly batting with white backing, fits double bed. $345.00

205689 – TOP RIGHT: 9-PATCH; 43" x 43"; dusty rose, blue & brown; cotton blend; made in Kentucky in 1989; machine pieced, hand quilted with polyester batting, matching floral blocks & borders. $190.00

305689 – CENTER LEFT: DAD'S ROSES; 60" x 60"; burgundy/green on muslin; cotton; made in Colorado in 1988; hand pieced, hand quilted; roses, drawn then cut for different pattern pieces, took 86 hours to quilt. $920.00

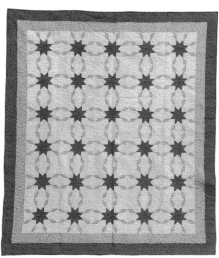

405689 – CENTER: BLAZING STAR; 80" x 96"; matching blue prints; cotton & cotton polyester; made in Indiana in 1988; hand pieced, machine quilted; polyester batting, washable, all new fabric. $156.00

505689 – CENTER RIGHT: SUNBONNET GIRL; 72" x 85"; navy blue with matching print; cotton & cotton/polyester; made in Indiana in 1988; machine quilted, hand appliqued; all new material, washable, all new material. $144.00

605689 – BOTTOM LEFT: LOG CABIN; 100" x 116"; dusty rose & brown prints; polyester blend; hand quilted, machine pieced. $230.00

705689 – BOTTOM RIGHT: BROKEN STAR; 83" x 94"; burgundy, tan & blue; top is 100% cotton, backing is poly-cotton blend; made in Louisiana in 1989; machine pieced, hand quilted; washable with low-loft poly batting, quilt has won Best of Show at local fair. $575.00

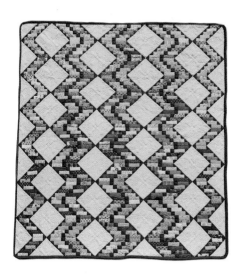

106689 – TOP LEFT: TRIP AROUND THE WORLD; 76" x 96"; blue, red & beige; 100% cotton; made in Vermont in 1988; machine pieced, tied; made using Eleanor Burns Quilt-In-A-Day method. $259.00

206689 – TOP RIGHT: SCRAP QUILT; 80" x 92"; baby blue, navy & blue scrap; cottons/blends; made in Oregon in 1982; machine pieced, hand quilted; made by a Mennonite lady. $432.00

306689 – CENTER LEFT: LONE STAR; 94" x 108"; dusty blue & peach with off-white background; cotton & polyester/cotton; made in Missouri in 1989; machine pieced, hand quilted; made by Mennonites. $432.00

406689 – CENTER: SCRAPBAG FAN; 78" x 88"; multi-color set with rose & yellow; blends; made in Kentucky in 1988; hand & machine

pieced, hand quilted; close quilting, polyester batting, very colorful, pre-washed muslin backing. $230.00

506689 – CENTER RIGHT: 8-POINT STARS; 73" x 90"; fall colors on muslin; cotton; made in 1880's; hand pieced, hand quilted; beautifully quilted with cotton seed still visible in the batting. $230.00

606689 – BOTTOM LEFT: NINE PATCH; 72" x 72"; yellow & variegated prints; cotton & poly blends; made in Kentucky; hand pieced, hand quilted; polyester batting, machine washable. $144.00

706689 – BOTTOM RIGHT: BROKEN STAR; 98" x 110"; blue, gold, yellow & white with some print; made in 1986; machine pieced, hand quilted. $575.00

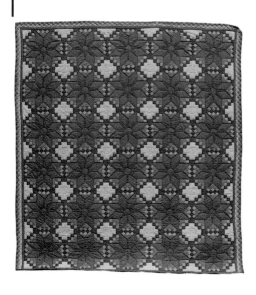

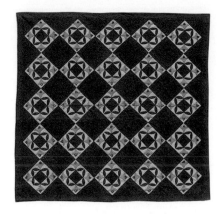

107689 – TOP LEFT: TULIPS; 80" x 80"; gray, white, gold & red; cotton; made in New York in 1880; hand pieced, hand quilted, hand appliqued; very thin batting, attractive gray print with gold & red tulips, quilted feather wreath in alternating blocks, good condition except small center of tulip fabric deteriorating, red & gold tulip fabric dates c. 1850. $374.00

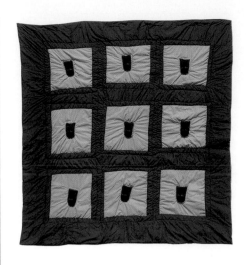

207689 – TOP RIGHT: CROWN ROYALE; 88" x 88"; purple & gold; hand quilted; has 9 Crown Royale sacks in center blocks. $403.00

307689 – CENTER LEFT: OUTBURST OF JOY; 50" x 54"; black with red, pink & purple; 100% cotton; made in Wisconsin in 1983; machine pieced, hand quilted; bold adaptation of a traditional compass design, winner of many awards at art & quilt shows, lots of quilting. $460.00

407689 – CENTER: HEART SILVER WEDDING ANNIVERSARY; 77" x 91"; silver print with white; poly-blend cottons; made in Texas in 1984; machine pieced, hand quilted combined with "tied" quilting; center heart square embroidered with space for date & names if desired, guests names on white

squares, combination of "tied" & hand quilting used. $133.00

507689 – CENTER RIGHT: ROYAL STAR OF KANSAS; 82½" x 91"; dark & light mauves, blue & green; all cottons, polyester batting; made in Indiana in 1989; machine pieced, hand quilted; never used, feathers & feathered hearts surround the star, cross hatch quilting in border, backing is light mauve print, signed & dated on back. $432.00

607689 – BOTTOM LEFT: CAJUN PRIM ROSE; 77" X 94"; dark & light green with rose & pink primrose on mint green block; cotton & cotton blends; made in Louisiana in 1989; machine pieced, hand quilted; rose & pink Cajun primrose accents the mint green center block of the dark & light green print, Double Irish Chain pattern. $633.00

707689 – BOTTOM RIGHT: NORTH CAROLINA LILY; 82" x 96"; burgundy, teal; top & back are poly-cotton blends; made in Louisiana in 1988; won 1st Place at local fair, poly lowloft batting, machine washable. $489.00

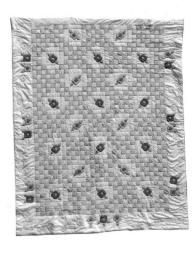

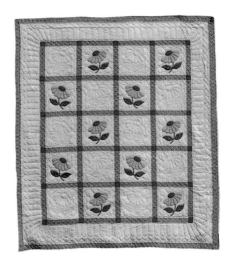

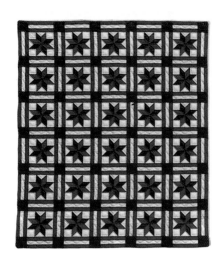

108689 – TOP LEFT: YELLOW DAISY; 86" x 101"; white with yellow, orange & green; cotton/cotton poly blend; made in New York in 1979; hand quilted, hand appliqued; quilted with yellow thread, won a ribbon at New York State Fair, never used. $460.00

208689 – TOP RIGHT: BICENTENNIAL; 86" x 101"; red, white & blue print; made in Indiana in 1985; poly-cotton; machine pieced, hand quilted; white lining, polyester batting. $374.00

308689 – CENTER LEFT: DOGWOOD; 78" x 94"; green, brown & white; cotton, made in 1930's; hand quilted; appliqued with spider web pattern, quilted in large open areas. $575.00

408689 – CENTER: LOG CABIN HEART; 82" x 84"; blues; cotton & cotton blends; made in Utah in 1988; machine pieced, machine

quilted; nice large wall quilt or nice lap quilt, quilting is done with hearts. $173.00

508689 – CENTER RIGHT: OGEE; 79" x 98½"; navy & white; cotton; made in Utah in 1988; machine pieced & quilted; quilting done in rose pattern, an ogee is an s-curve. $173.00

608689 – BOTTOM LEFT: LOG CABIN; 78" x 92"; pink, brown & red; 100% cotton, except brown & red are polyester/cotton; made in Vermont in 1987; machine pieced, tied; quilt made using Eleanor Burns' Quilt-A-Day method, sewn for warmth & comfort. $230.00

708689 – BOTTOM RIGHT: DIAMOND STAR LOG CABIN; 85" x 102"; shades of blue; polyester/cotton; made in Ohio in 1988; machine pieced, hand quilted; dark to light colors gives the star a 3-dimensional look. $489.00

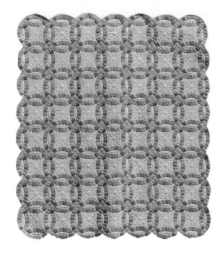

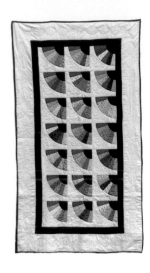

109689 – TOP LEFT: DOUBLE WEDDING RING; 83" x 97"; blues & tans with cream background; polyester/cotton; made in Ohio in 1988; machine pieced, hand quilted. $489.00

209689 – TOP RIGHT: RAINBOW FAN; 57" x 104"; yellow, green, blue, purple, pink, red & black fans/black sash/white background; 100% cottons & poly-cottons, made in Louisiana in 1988; machine pieced, hand quilted; pre-washed, extra long for generous pillow tuck, small black check backing, polyester batting, made by French Cajun. $230.00

309689 – CENTER LEFT: OHIO STAR; 82" x 96"; red & white; 100% cotton; made in Kentucky in 1988; hand pieced; quilting follows outline of star, feather wreath in plain block. $345.00

409689 – CENTER: DOUBLE WEDDING RING; 86" x 98"; all colors with corner square green & peach; all cotton; made in Kansas in 1989; machine pieced, hand quilted; design

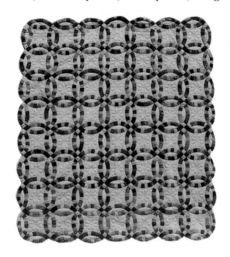

quilted in plain blocks, beige background, white backing. $414.00

509689 – CENTER RIGHT: CLAY'S CHOICE; 72" x 93"; red, white & blue; cotton & cotton blends; made in Louisiana in 1988; machine pieced, hand quilted; old looking prints of red, white & blue gives old look, made by Cajun lady. $403.00

609689 – BOTTOM LEFT: TRIP AROUND THE WORLD; 86" x 100"; light to dark; all cotton; made in Alabama in 1988; machine pieced, hand quilted; sheet lining, double quilted. $403.00

709689 – BOTTOM RIGHT: COUNTRY PATCHWORK; 72" x 74"; variegated prints & solids; polyester; made in Kentucky in 1987; hand pieced, hand quilted; multi-purpose quilts, made of good polyester knits, seams embellished with embroidery stitch, makes beautiful table cloth or wallhanging, all hand work, poly padding, machine washable. $202.00

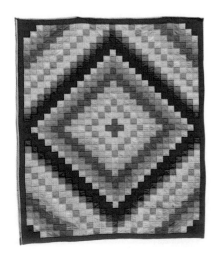

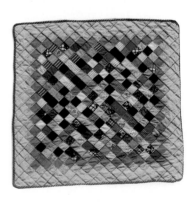

110689 – TOP LEFT: "BLUE BASKETS"; 88" x 105"; blue & off-white, rose bow; made in Wisconsin in 1989; hand & machine pieced, hand quilted; very soft looking with quilted bouquets of flowers in blank squares, quilted cable & feathers in border. $549.00

210689 – TOP RIGHT: DOUBLE WEDDING RING; 94" x 96"; soft prints; all cotton; made in Alabama in 1988; machine pieced, hand quilted; white sheet lining, double quilting, blue & yellow predominant colors. $403.00

310689 – CENTER LEFT: OHIO ROSE; 78" x 97"; green, pink & white; cotton; made in 1988; hand quilted, hand appliqued. $345.00

410689 – CENTER: DIAMOND BUTTERFLY; 83" x 103"; brown & cream; cotton/polyester blend; made in Ohio in 1985; hand pieced, hand quilted; quilted butterfly setting in diamond center with dogwood flowers in

square bordered with sawtooth strips, cream backing, quilted with peach thread, polyester batting. $374.00

510689 – CENTER RIGHT: ABC QUILT; 90" x 92"; pink, blue & white; cotton; made in Indiana in 1920's; hand quilted; each block has in it a letter of the alphabet. $633.00

610689 – BOTTOM LEFT: FLOWER GARDEN; 88" x 102"; variety of colors, brown with small dots in centers; cottons & poly-cottons; made in Indiana in 1988; hand pieced, hand quilted; permanent press unbleached for background & lining, polyester batting, binding of small blue print, won 1st prize in quilt show in 1988. $512.00

710689 – BOTTOM RIGHT: FLOWER GARDEN BLOCK; 88" x 98"; assorted colors, un-bleached muslin with brown border; cotton blends; made in Arkansas in 1983; hand & machine pieced, hand quilted. $259.00

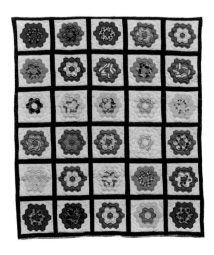

111689 – TOP LEFT: SISTER'S CHOICE; 80" x 90"; cream, blue, mauve; 100% cotton; made in Wisconsin in 1988; machine pieced, hand quilted; lightweight polyester 100% batting, heavily quilted, signed & dated. Price includes matching 42" x 42" wallhanging. $460.00

211689 – TOP RIGHT: LONE STAR; 88" x 104"; rose & maroon; cotton & cotton-polyester; made in Kansas in 1987; machine pieced, hand quilted; 3 shades of maroon & rose, polyester batting, sheet lining. $386.00

311689 – CENTER LEFT: DOUBLE WEDDING RING; 72" x 78"; hand quilted, some stains. $345.00

411689 – CENTER: INDIAN TRAILS; 72" x 96"; white, blue & yellow; cotton top; top machine pieced in Iowa c. 1927, quilted & bound in Arkansas in 1988; machine pieced, hand quilted; old-time fabrics like flour sacking, polyfil batting, each piece outline

quilted & a double line of diamonds quilted in sashes & borders. $213.00

511689 – CENTER RIGHT: COURTHOUSE STEPS; 72" x 83"; white & red; polyester & cotton; made in Kentucky & Illinois in 1986; machine pieced, hand quilted. $179.00

611689 – BOTTOM LEFT: APPLIQUED BUTTERFLY; 73" x 93"; brown; cotton/-polyester; made in Missouri in 1987; hand quilted, machine appliqued; polyester fill. $230.00

711689 – BOTTOM RIGHT: DOUBLE WEDDING RING; 76" x 84"; multi-color prints with white background; cotton-poly; made in Missouri in 1988; machine pieced, hand quilted; hand quilted around each piece with double bells in center, white lining & binding. $345.00

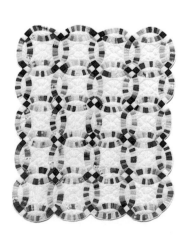

112689 – TOP LEFT: BEAR CLAW; 68" x 84"; black/lt. aqua; cotton & cotton/poly; made in Arkansas in 1986; machine pieced, hand quilted; polyfil batting, back is tiny print that contains the colors of the top & binding, each piece is outline stitched, bear claws are hand quilted in the borders, all quilting is done in black thread, Amish-type design & colors, never used. $213.00

212689 – TOP RIGHT: BASKET; 69" x 80"; antique pink & tan; cotton; made in Indiana c. 1900; machine pieced, hand quilted; rare back "watered silk" (cotton) black & red print, never used. $1,380.00

312689 – CENTER LEFT: "EAGLE"; 44" x 45"; red, gold, dk. blue, lt. blue; cotton/poly-cotton; made in Wisconsin in 1989; wallhanging, royal blue backing. $87.00

412689 – CENTER: PINWHEEL; 42" x 42"; bright & pastel colors on off-white background; cotton & cotton blends; made in Louisiana in 1989; "old-time" bright & pastel

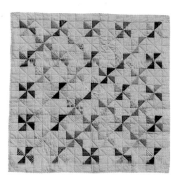

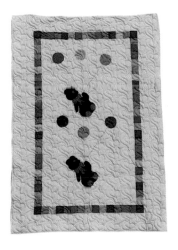

pinwheels on off-white background "like Grandma use to make," can be used as wallhanging or crib quilt. $115.00

512689 – CENTER RIGHT: TEDDY BEARS AND BALLOONS; 40" x 60"; brown bears with multi-color balloons on cream; cotton/blend; made in Missouri in 1988; machine appliqued & quilted; heart design quilting, Dacron fill, new, washable, very practical. $58.00

612689 – BOTTOM LEFT: SAMPLER; 39" x 39"; brown, cream & blue; cotton & polyester; made in Minnesota in 1985; hand pieced, quilted & appliqued; 4 traditional patterns, print border, signed, heavily quilted with cream thread, may be used as bed topper, table cover or wallhanging. $144.00

712689 – BOTTOM RIGHT: BOW TIE; 33" x 40"; polished cotton & cotton blends; made in Indiana in 1988; machine pieced, hand quilted; signed & dated. $87.00

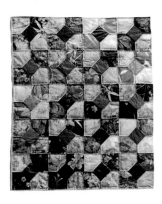

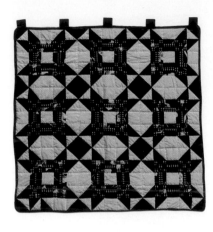

113689 – TOP LEFT: INTERLOCKED SQUARES; 32" x 32"; rust & brown; cotton & polyester; made in Minnesota in 1985; hand pieced, hand quilted; pieced border, heavily quilted, suitable for wallhanging, bed topper or table cover. $87.00

213689 – TOP RIGHT: MISSOURI PUZZLE; 44" x 46"; black & white; poly-cotton; made in Missouri in 1988; machine pieced, hand quilted; solid & prints, black lining, quilted with black thread, quilted around each piece. $115.00

313689 – CENTER LEFT: MARTHA'S MOUNTAIN MEDALLION; 47" x 47"; composed of patchwork & hand applique; blue ribbon winner in Minnesota quilt show. $183.00

413689 – CENTER: RIBBONED GLORY; 42" x 42"; lt. & dk. greens, peach & lavender; cotton/poly; made in Washington in 1988; hand pieced & quilted; stars set in ribbon-like

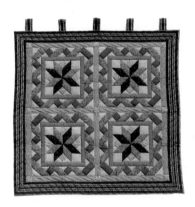

setting, contrast cable quilting on sashing, wonderful blend of greens & peach with a touch of lavender. $115.00

513689 – CENTER RIGHT: HEARTS AROUND THE WORLD; 42" x 54"; pink prints; cottons & blends; made in North Carolina in 1985; machine quilted & appliqued; soft fabrics, machine quilted heart in each square, print backing. $87.00

613689 – BOTTOM LEFT: LONE STAR; 45" x 45"; mauves & tans; all cotton; made in Indiana in 1989; machine pieced, hand quilted; all solid colors, quilted around each diamond, circle quilting around star, basket weave border, signed & dated. $138.00

713689 – BOTTOM RIGHT: CHECKERBOARD HEARTS; 25" x 32"; pink & off-white; cottons & cotton blends; made in North Dakota in 1988; machine pieced & quilted; simple, country-style wall quilt or bassinet-sized baby quilt. $46.00

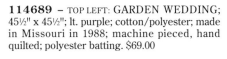

114689 – TOP LEFT: GARDEN WEDDING; 45½" x 45½"; lt. purple; cotton/polyester; made in Missouri in 1988; machine pieced, hand quilted; polyester batting. $69.00

214689 – TOP RIGHT: ROAMING STRIPE; 26" x 33"; multi-colored fabrics & muslin; cottons & blends; made in North Carolina; machine pieced & quilted; colorful piece, quilted in the ditch around each square, blue backing. $69.00

314689 – CENTER LEFT: MEDALLION; 45" x 54"; brown, deep green, peach flowers, white birds & flowers, green leaves; all cotton; made in North Carolina in 1980; machine pieced, hand quilted; oriental flowers, birds & trees, beautiful colors, center panel pre-printed; quilted leaves in center border. $144.00

414689 – CENTER: ROCKING HORSE; 40" x 60"; cream, red check gingham; cotton/blend; made in Missouri in 1988; machine applique, machine quilted; quilted clover-leaf design, Dacron fill, washable, very practical. $46.00

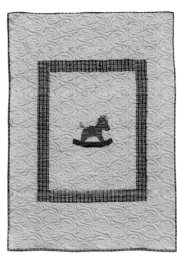

514689 – CENTER RIGHT: THE EARTH RECEIVES THE SEED; 65" x 65"; black/solids & prints; cotton, blends, challis; made in California in 1984; machine pieced, hand quilted; cotton classic batting, inspired by bleakness of winter's earth, but knowing that in due time blossoms would come forth again. $736.00

614689 – BOTTOM LEFT: CHRISTMAS; 49½" x 49½"; red, green & white; 100% cottons; made in Colorado in 1988; hand pieced, quilted & appliqued; lively Christmas sampler that will bring cheer to all who see it. $230.00

714689 – BOTTOM RIGHT: OVERALL SAM; 40" x 45"; lt. blue, royal blue, reds, greens & yellows; poly cotton & cotton fabric; made in Wisconsin in 1989; hand embroidered & appliqued, machine pieced & quilted; royal blue backing, double batting, perfect for little boy. $87.00

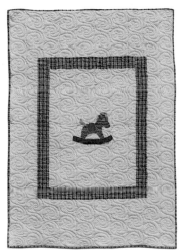

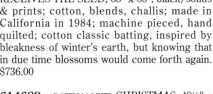

115689 – TOP LEFT: TRIP AROUND THE WORLD; 41" x 44"; multi-colored; cotton & polyester blend; made in Illinois in 1988; machine pieced, hand quilted; bright colors will cheer any room, each square measures ¾". $58.00

215689 – TOP RIGHT: IMAGE OF SPRING; 39" x 41"; cream/green/lavender/brown; cotton/-flannel inner lining; made in California in 1979; hand pieced & quilted. $432.00

315689 – CENTER LEFT: INDIAN RUG; 33" x 45"; black; all cotton; made in Illinois in 1987; machine pieced, hand quilted; pre-washed fabric, polyester batting, signed & dated, sleeve for hanging, quilting design is original sunburst & thunderbird pattern. $100.00

415689 – CENTER: BABY BLOCKS; 40" x 52"; teal, pink & cream; 100% top quality cottons; made in Colorado in 1987; machine pieced,

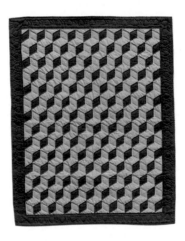

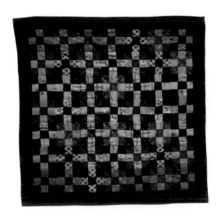

hand quilted; old Baby Blocks pattern completed with a heart quilted border. $202.00

515689 – CENTER RIGHT: NINE-PATCH LATTICE; 24" x 24"; red & blue; cottons; made in North Dakota in 1988; machine pieced & quilted; wallhanging, placement of lights & darks make it appear to have a light lattice over a dark background. $30.00

615689 – BOTTOM LEFT: A HEART OF A BEAR; 43" x 44"; red, brown, beige; all cotton; made in Illinois in 1988; hand quilted; pre-washed, polyester batting, quilting done in red thread, quilted design of hearts, figures are part of fabric (not appliqued). $71.00

715689 – BOTTOM RIGHT: DINOSAUR WALLHANGING; 24" x 28"; gold & green; poly-blend cottons; made in Texas in 1989; hand appliqued & quilted; dinosaur stands 15" tall & is of green calico print, rod pocket for 1" rod attached to back. $35.00

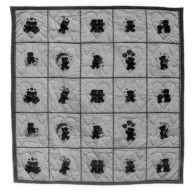

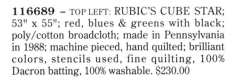

116689 – TOP LEFT: RUBIC'S CUBE STAR; 53" x 55"; red, blues & greens with black; poly/cotton broadcloth; made in Pennsylvania in 1988; machine pieced, hand quilted; brilliant colors, stencils used, fine quilting, 100% Dacron batting, 100% washable. $230.00

216689 – TOP RIGHT: BOW TIE; 62½" x 80½"; red/teal; cotton; made in Kentucky in 1935; hand pieced & quilted; older quilt with mixed color bow ties enclosed in a gray stripe, squares set together with red & teal. $230.00

316689 – CENTER LEFT: ROMAN STRIPE; 74" x 86"; terra cotta & turquoise with red; cotton; made in 1988; machine pieced, hand tied; double batt (Mountain Mist) & ecru flannel sheet blanket on back, never used. $230.00

416689 – CENTER: LOG CABIN VARIATION; 75½" x 83"; mixed gray/blue/burgundy; cotton; made in Kentucky c. 1930; hand pieced

& quilted; older multi-color Log Cabin variation with assorted colors, some fading on border, some worn spots. $403.00

516689 – CENTER RIGHT: HEARTS & GIZZARDS; 82" x 96"; yellow & white; cotton blends; made in Ohio in 1988; machine pieced, hand quilted; polyester batting, never used. $259.00

616689 – BOTTOM LEFT: YORK ROSE; 80" x 92"; navy blue, wine, wine print on beige; cotton & cotton blend; made in Ohio in 1988; hand pieced & quilted; large roses blend in with color scheme. $460.00

716689 – BOTTOM RIGHT: DRESDEN PLATE; 72" x 87"; multi-color; cotton; made in Pennsylvania in 1940; machine pieced, hand quilted & appliqued. $288.00

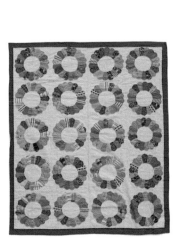

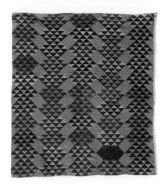

117689 – TOP LEFT: FLYING GEESE; 66" x 72"; blue with red & white calico; cotton; made in New York c. 1910; hand pieced & quilted; interesting combination of triangles. $305.00

217689 – TOP RIGHT: "GARNET" adaptation of Churn Dash block; 94" x 94"; rose & barn reds with cornflower blue; 100% cottons & 1 poly-cotton fabric; top made in Florida, quilted in Arkansas in 1986; machine pieced, hand quilted; evolution of Churn Dash "Nine Patch" in center & Ohio Star using repeat stripes for a centralized design, Cotton Classic™ batting, never used. $920.00

317689 – CENTER LEFT: PHILADELPHIA BEAUTY; 75" x 80"; rose, pink, red & white; cotton; made in Pennsylvania c. 1900; hand quilted & appliqued; unusual pattern. $328.00

417689 – CENTER: AMISH PLAIN QUILT; 68" x 80"; blue & white; cotton; made in 1920's; machine pieced, hand quilted; old-order Swartzentruber Amish quilt, elaborate

feathered wreaths, tulips, hearts & trailing vines, 2 small wear spots on white, reversible side is pale blue. $460.00

517689 – CENTER RIGHT: ROYAL STAR OF GEORGIA; 90" x 94"; dark rose, pink & burgundy; cotton polyester; made in Missouri in 1988; machine pieced, hand quilted; one in a series of Royal Stars Of The States, white fill with white lining, extra plump polyester batting. $345.00

617689 – BOTTOM LEFT: DOUBLE WEDDING RING; 90" x 103"; multi-color cream fill; cotton/polyester; made in Missouri in 1988; machine pieced, hand quilted; polyester batting. $345.00

717689 – BOTTOM RIGHT: SUNSHINE AND SHADOWS; 95" x 103"; clear plain colors in 3 shades of each; 65% poly/35% cotton broad-cloth; made in Pennsylvania in 1988; machine pieced, hand quilted; made by Amish grandmother, stencils used, dated. $460.00

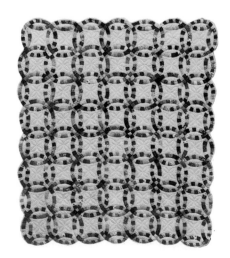

118689 – TOP LEFT: UNKNOWN; 73" x 78"; white on white; cotton; made in 1921; looks like a wedding quilt, exquisitely embroidered & quilted, flowers, animals, birds, etc., photo is close-up attempt to show some of the handwork,initialed & dated, has pillow sham. $1,529.00

218689 – TOP RIGHT: BRIAR ROSE; 82" x 102"; lt. blue & ivory; cotton blend; made in 1987; hand pieced & quilted; some call this pattern Cherokee Rose. $575.00

318689 – CENTER LEFT: DAHLIA; 96" x 110"; dusty blue; cotton/poly; made in Missouri in 1989; machine pieced, hand quilted; Dacron batting, Mennonite made, signed & dated. $420.00

418689 – CENTER: DOUBLE WEDDING RING; 106" x 106"; multi-color with cream fill; cotton-polyester; made in Missouri in 1988;

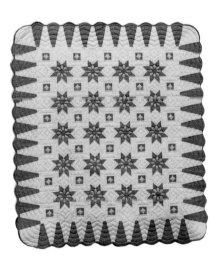

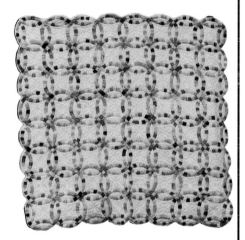

machine pieced, hand quilted; polyester batting. $345.00

518689 – CENTER RIGHT: DRESDEN PLATE; 88" x 106"; blue; cotton & cotton polyester; made in Kansas in 1989; machine pieced, hand quilted & appliqued; plates are a mixed color scheme, sheet lining, poly batt (Mountain Mist). $385.00

618689 – BOTTOM LEFT: DOUBLE WEDDING RING; 107" x 107"; multi-color ; cotton/polyester; made in Missouri in 1988; machine pieced, hand quilted; white background, polyester fill. $345.00

718689 – BOTTOM RIGHT: BROKEN STAR; 72" x 92"; dk. green & white; poly-cotton broadcloth; made in Missouri in 1989; machine pieced, hand quilted; quilted on both sides of seam, Fatt Batt or Comfort Weight batting, poly-cotton muslin sheet lining, signed & dated. $230.00

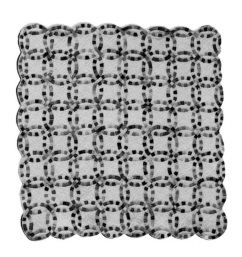

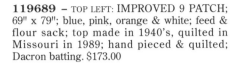

119689 – TOP LEFT: IMPROVED 9 PATCH; 69" x 79"; blue, pink, orange & white; feed & flour sack; top made in 1940's, quilted in Missouri in 1989; hand pieced & quilted; Dacron batting. $173.00

219689 – TOP RIGHT: STAR DAHLIA; 102" x 102"; peach, dusty green; cotton & polyester-cotton; made in Missouri, machine pieced, hand quilted; Mennonite-made, off-white background. $460.00

319689 –CENTER LEFT: GRANDMOTHER'S FAN; 85" x 98"; brown & tan; all cotton; made in Kansas in 1985; machine pieced, hand quilted & appliqued; lace-trimmed around each fan. $374.00

419689 – CENTER: NINE PATCH VARI-ATION; 66" x 88"; red, white & blue; cotton; made in New York in 1920; hand pieced & quilted; muslin on back. $357.00

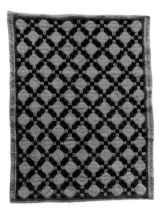

519689 – CENTER RIGHT: BUTTERFLY PARADISE; 79" x 91"; multi-color butterflies; cotton-blend; made in Idaho in 1988; machine pieced, hand quilted & appliqued; butterflies around wild roses, lots of hand quilting in pink area, Mountain Mist batting. $345.00

619689 – BOTTOM LEFT: SAILS; 41" x 56"; lt. blue, navy with white & mauve sailboats; 100% cottons; made in Pennsylvania in 1988; machine pieced, hand quilted & appliqued; Fairfield 100% bonded polyester batting, 100% unbleached muslin backing, never used. $161.00

719689 – BOTTOM RIGHT: U.S. PRESIDENTS; 90" x 108"; red, white & blue; polyester cotton blend; made in Washington in 1988; hand quilted & embroidered; last 40 presidents, actual eye & hair color, very detailed. $748.00

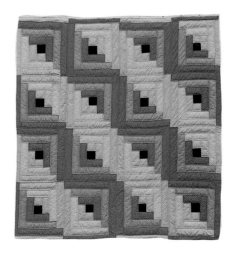

101989 – TOP LEFT: LOG CABIN; 72" x 81"; rose & pink; cotton & cotton blends; made in Arkansas in 1988; machine pieced, hand quilted. $230.00

201989 – TOP RIGHT: STAR CROSSED HEARTS; 51" x 51"; rose, lavender & green; cotton; made in Pennsylvania in 1986; machine pieced, hand quilted; polyester batting, signed & dated, wall-hanging has sleeve on back. $207.00

301989 – CENTER LEFT: SCRAP; 72" x 81"; all colors; cottons; made in Oklahoma in 1930's, quilted in 1987; machine pieced, hand quilted by the piece; unbleached backing; zigzag edges on side & straight borders on ends. $173.00

401989 – CENTER: OLD MAID'S PUZZLE; 60" x 60"; mauves & bronzes; cotton; made in New Jersey in 1988; machine pieced, hand quilted. $230.00

501989 – CENTER RIGHT: CARPENTERS WHEEL; 88" x 92"; burgundy, grays, muslin; 100% cotton; made in Washington in 1987; hand pieced, hand quilted. $949.00

601989 – BOTTOM LEFT: STRING QUILT, 73" x 83"; old shirt & dress materials; made in Georgia; top hand pieced by male slave from Georgia c. 1860, hand quilted in 1940, slight wear on top. $230.00

701989 – BOTTOM RIGHT: 9 PATCH; 68" x 78"; cotton; hand pieced, hand quilted; some fabrics dating back to 1800's. $575.00

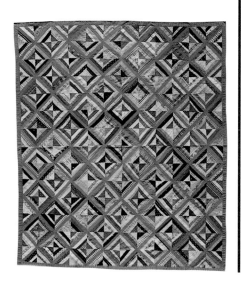

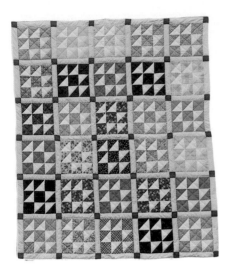

102989 – TOP LEFT: DOUBLE X; 71" x 84"; varied colors, prints & solids; cotton & cotton blends; made in Arkansas in 1988; machine pieced, hand quilted; double bias binding. $230.00

202989 – TOP RIGHT: MOC LOG CABIN; 80" x 80"; multi-colored; 100% cottons; made in Wisconsin in 1988; machine pieced & quilted; poly batting. $460.00

302989 – CENTER LEFT: TEXAS LONE STAR; 80" x 88"; small prints & solids with light blue, yellow & gold with orange accents; cotton-poly blends; made in Appalachia in 1971; hand pieced & quilted; has been washed, some of the orange color has spotted the white in a few places. $460.00

402989 – CENTER: UNION SQUARE BEAR PAW; 55" x 55"; cranberry red, green & natural; cotton muslin, solids; made in Iowa in 1988; machine pieced, hand quilted; lowloft polyfil batt. $69.00

502989 – CENTER RIGHT: SUNBON-NET SUE; 72" x 87"; poly blends; machine appliqued & pieced, hand quilted; poly blend print dresses on muslin, light blue sashing, gold & yellow check corner squares, yellow lining & binding. $156.00

602989 – BOTTOM LEFT: BANBURY CROSS; 76" x 98"; brown, mauve, burgundy, greens & off-white; poly-cotton blend; made in Ohio in 1985; machine pieced, hand quilted; polyester batting. $460.00

702989 – BOTTOM RIGHT: SUMMER WINDOW; 88" x 107"; multi-colors; cotton/cotton blends; made in 1986; hand applique, hand quilted; original picture quilt designed from hayfield & mountains, rainbow in sky surrounded by flowers of satin, bias tape to resemble stain glass, polyester batting. $1,035.00

103989 – TOP LEFT: 8-POINTED STARS; 69" x 80"; brown & rust stars with terra cotta sashing; 100% cotton; made in Wisconsin in 1989; machine pieced, hand quilted; poly batting. $432.00

203989 – TOP RIGHT: MAPLE LEAF; 84" x 92"; green & white, leaves are red, green, yellow & brown prints; cotton & cotton blends; made in Missouri in 1981; hand pieced, quilted & appliqued. $391.00

303989 – CENTER LEFT: LONE STAR; 92" x 98"; pastels & cream; cotton, cotton blends; made in North Carolina & Virginia in 1989; machine pieced, hand quilted; pastel print backing with solid blue border & binding, bonded poly batting, signed & dated. $345.00

403989 – CENTER: LOG CABIN #2; 24"

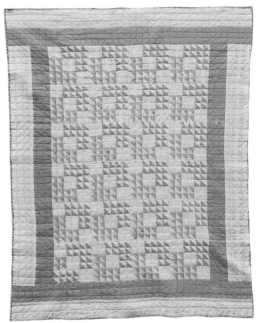

x 24"; 100% cotton, cotton batting; made in Texas in 1989; machine pieced, hand quilted; coordinating greens & pinks with heart quilting in border. $115.00

503989 – CENTER RIGHT: BROKEN GLASS; 74" x 92"; coral & light blue print; cotton & cotton blends; made in Louisiana in 1989; machine pieced, hand quilted. $403.00

603989 – BOTTOM LEFT: BEAR IN THE MOON; 40" x 60"; brown, orange & blue on cream; cotton & blend applique; made in Missouri in 1989; machine quilted & appliqued; Dacron fill, washable. $55.00

703989 – BOTTOM RIGHT: STAR PUZ-ZLE; 90" x 106"; peach, dark brown & blue; cotton; made in South Dakota in 1988; machine pieced, hand quilted. $460.00

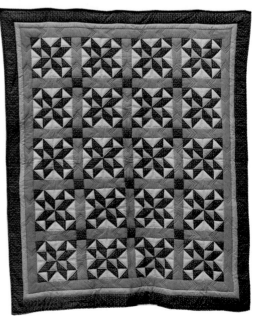

98

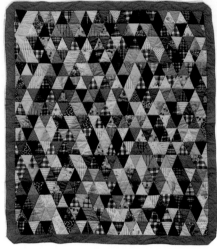

104989 – TOP LEFT: PYRAMID; 78" x 91"; multi-color; cotton & cotton blends; made in Arkansas in 1989; machine pieced, hand quilted. $230.00

204989 – TOP RIGHT: JACOB'S LADDER VARIATION; 84" x 108"; blue & pink; cotton; made in Nevada in 1989; machine pieced, hand quilted; polyester bonded batting, washed. $399.00

304989 – CENTER LEFT: GRANDMOTHER'S FAN; 81" x 97"; pink, black & white; cotton & cotton blends; made in Arkansas in 1988; hand & machine pieced, hand quilted; double bias binding. $259.00

404989 – CENTER: CRAZY QUILT; 89" x 101"; multi-color; cotton percale & sateen & flannel; made in Michigan in

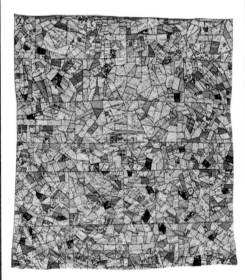

1920's or 30's; quilt is tied & stabilized. $575.00

504989 – CENTER RIGHT: CHERRY TREE; 86" x 110"; off-white background with green leaves & stems, red cherries; cotton blends; made in Kentucky in 1977; appliqued, hand quilted; "cherries" are actual little balls of cloth. $1,380.00

604989 – BOTTOM LEFT: ANTIQUE CARS; 72" x 90"; white & navy blue; cotton percale; made in Georgia in 1989; machine pieced, hand quilted, cross stitched; polyester lining. $575.00

704989 – BOTTOM RIGHT: LOG CABIN; 81" x 96"; brown, orange, off-white, red; cotton polyester blends; made in Idaho in 1989; machine pieced, hand quilted; Mountain Mist batting. $345.00

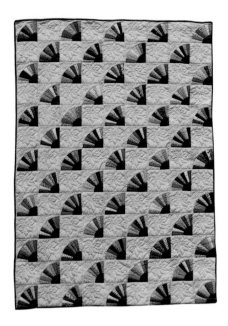

105989 – TOP LEFT: GRANDMOTHER'S FAN; 71" x 100"; beige, brown, assorted prints; cotton; made in Pennsylvania in 1989; machine pieced, hand quilted; beige backing with brown binding. $230.00

205989 – TOP RIGHT: WINDOWS OF REMINISCENCE; 80" x 90"; black, pinks, greens; silk, acetate, cotton, rayon; made in West Virginia in 1986; hand & machine pieced & hand quilted; reversible. $575.00

305989 – CENTER LEFT: DOUBLE WEDDING RING; 84" x 96"; blue; polyester & cotton; made in 1986; hand pieced & quilted; backing is natural, polyester & cotton, batting is 100% Mountain Mist polyester. $460.00

405989 – CENTER: TRIP AROUND THE WORLD; 58" x 72"; green/white;

cotton poly blend; made in 1989; machine pieced, no quilting; this is a biscuit quilt each stuffed by hand, lined with white cotton sheet which is barr tacked to front, polyfil stuffing. $115.00

505989 – CENTER RIGHT: SAMPLER QUILT; 90" x 110"; brown & natural; cotton & cotton blends; made in 1989; machine pieced, hand quilted & appliqued. $385.00

605989 – BOTTOM LEFT: A CHRISTMAS COVERING; 41" x 57"; red, green & white Christmas prints; cotton & few cotton blends; made in Illinois in 1989; machine pieced, hand quilted. $161.00

705989 – BOTTOM RIGHT: MEXICAN STAR; 86" x 91"; blue, maroon & beige; cotton & cotton blends; made in Arkansas in 1987; machine pieced, hand quilted. $397.00

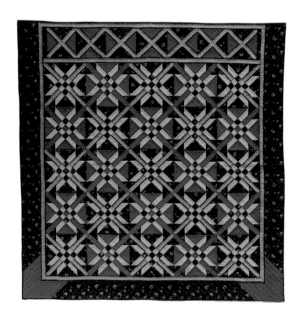

106989 – TOP LEFT: CLAY'S CHOICE; 84" x 97"; dusty rose print & solid; cotton; made in New Jersey in 1988; machine pieced, hand quilted. $403.00

206989 – TOP RIGHT: POTTED CACTUS; 75" x 95"; green, beige, pink & yellow; cotton & cotton blends; made in Arkansas in 1988; hand & machine pieced, hand quilted; polyester batting, cotton blend backing. $247.00

306989 – CENTER LEFT: SHOO-FLY; 88" x 88"; greens; mostly cotton; made in Delaware; hand pieced, primitive hand quilting. $150.00

406989 – CENTER: STRING; 62" x 79"; mixture of different colors; cotton; made in Kentucky in 1940; hand pieced, hand quilted; primitive. $288.00

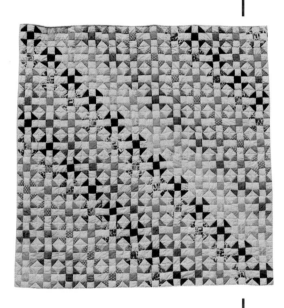

506989 – CENTER RIGHT: EMBROIDERED FLOWERS; 90" x 102"; yellow & green embroidery on gold & white framing; cotton; made in Montana in 1985; hand quilted; backing is white muslin, polyester batting. $345.00

606989 – BOTTOM LEFT: LOG CABIN PATTERN; 78" x 98"; red, brown & blue prints; cotton; made in Colorado in 1988; machine pieced, machine quilted; 100% polyester extra loft batting, binding is double thickness. $276.00

706989 – BOTTOM RIGHT: SHELL; 83" x 87"; variegated pink & solids; cotton/polyester; made in Missouri in 1989; machine pieced, hand quilted; extra fluffy Dacron batting, parement lining, fabric is doubled on binding. $288.00

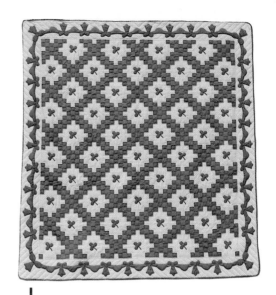

107989 – TOP LEFT: NINE-PATCH; 72" x 80"; navy & pink; cotton; made in Wyoming in 1988; machine pieced, tied; double batt & flannel backing. $196.00

207989 – TOP RIGHT: IRISH CHAIN; 79" x 88"; green & white; broadcloth; made in Illinois in 1989; machine pieced, hand appliqued & quilted. $345.00

307989 – CENTER LEFT: SQUARE PATCH; 60" x 85"; solids & plaids; wool; made in Missouri in 1989; machine pieced, hand tied; briar stitch around each block, red cotton flannel lined, Dacron batting. $173.00

407989 – CENTER: LOG CABIN - BARN RAISING; 58" x 72"; multi, mostly blue & red; cotton; made in Pennsylvania c. 1900; hand pieced, tied; each block made with ½" strips. $253.00

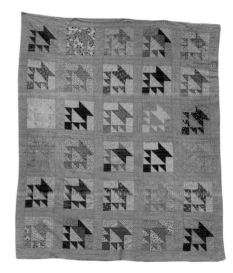

507989 – CENTER RIGHT: SUGAR BOWL; 69" x 82"; scraps on pink background; all cotton; made in Kansas in 1920's; machine pieced, hand quilted; soft, lightweight quilt, one tiny hole in border. $345.00

607989 – BOTTOM LEFT: WILDFLOWER AFTERNOON, A Drunkard's Path Variation; 84" x 107"; aqua, forest green & russet; cotton/poly blend; made in Washington in 1989; hand pieced & quilted; buttons in "cross" center. $403.00

707989 – BOTTOM RIGHT: UNKNOWN; 67" x 84"; multi-color & navy borders; cotton; made in Arkansas in 1970's; hand & machine pieced, hand quilted; polyester batting. $213.00

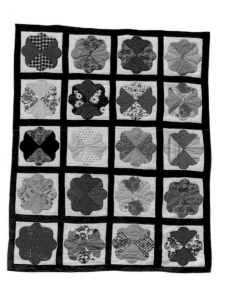

108989 – TOP LEFT: DOUBLE IRISH CHAIN; 78½" x 98"; light blue, print, muslin (unbleached); all cotton; made in Michigan in 1988; machine pieced, hand quilted; Mountain Mist Quilt Light batting, quilted in feathered hearts & cats & hearts on borders, 20 st./in. $690.00

208989 – TOP RIGHT: UNUSUAL FLOWER GARDEN; 65½" x 74"; varied colors; cotton; made in Tennessee c. 1930; hand pieced, hand quilted; set together with strips of blue calico, primitive. $288.00

308989 – CENTER LEFT: LOG CABIN IN BARN RAISING DESIGN; 91" x 106"; peach & green; poly/cotton; made in Ohio in 1989; machine pieced, hand quilted. $391.00

408989 – CENTER: LOST IN AUSTIN; 45" x 48"; pink, orange, yellow, white & purple; cotton & cotton blends; made in

California in 1988; machine pieced, hand quilted; bonded poly batting. $316.00

508989 – CENTER RIGHT: 9 PATCH; 30" x 30"; browns, blues & green; cotton blend; made in Pennsylvania in 1989; machine pieced, hand quilted; made by Amish grandmother from scraps. $98.00

608989 – BOTTOM LEFT: IRISH CHAIN; 88" x 102"; dark blue & beige with muslin; cotton; made in Tennessee in 1988; machine pieced, hand quilted; polyester batting, muslin backing, matching bias binding. $375.00

708989 – BOTTOM RIGHT: ENCIRCLED TULIP; 96" x 104"; rose with pink & white; all cotton; made in Kansas in 1989; machine pieced, hand quilted & appliqued; medallion quilt with large tulip surrounded by smaller ones, Mountain Mist batting. $477.00

109989 – TOP LEFT: LOVE RING; 88" x 96"; blue; cotton polyester; made in Missouri in 1989; machine pieced, hand quilted; also has wallhanging 36" x 36" to match, polyester batting. $403.00

209989 – TOP RIGHT: BASKET QUILT; 80" x 92"; green & beige; calico & chambray; made in Missouri in 1917; hand pieced & quilted. $460.00

309989 – CENTER LEFT: TUMBLIN' STAR; 98" x 98"; peach & blue; cotton; made in Alabama in 1988; machine pieced, hand quilted; peach lining, quilted on each side of seam. $403.00

409989 – CENTER: JACOB'S FAN; 72" x 102"; blues, pinks & muslin; cotton & blends; made in Mississippi in 1988;

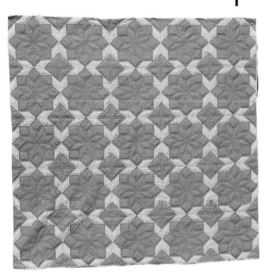

machine pieced, hand quilted; polyester batting, combination of Jacob's Ladder & Grandmother's Fan. $299.00

509989 – CENTER RIGHT: CRAZY QUILT; 72" x 84"; blacks, gray, tan, reds, maroons, plaids, etc; woolens, velveteens; made in Minnesota in 1880; hand pieced, machine quilted; no batting, embellishments in yarn, needs some restoration. $460.00

609989 – BOTTOM LEFT: FISH; 90" x 102"; cotton; made in Kentucky; hand pieced, hand quilted. $345.00

709989 – BOTTOM RIGHT: DUTCH GIRL; 66" x 80"; prints on white; cotton blends; made in Kentucky in 1988; hand quilted & appliqued; white lining, polyester batting. $201.00

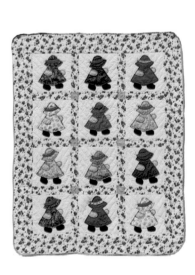

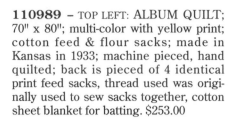

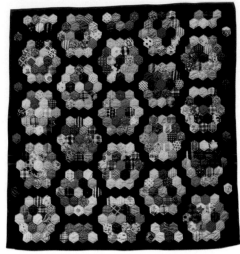

110989 – TOP LEFT: ALBUM QUILT; 70" x 80"; multi-color with yellow print; cotton feed & flour sacks; made in Kansas in 1933; machine pieced, hand quilted; back is pieced of 4 identical print feed sacks, thread used was originally used to sew sacks together, cotton sheet blanket for batting. $253.00

210989 – TOP RIGHT: GRANDMOTHER'S FLOWER GARDEN; 84" x 89"; prints & black; poly/cotton-cotton; made in Missouri in 1989; machine pieced, hand quilted; polyester bonded batting. $345.00

310989 – CENTER LEFT: EMBROIDERY BASKET OF FLOWERS; 90" x 108" before finishing; blue & white with embroidery; sheeting; made in Missouri in 1989; machine pieced, hand quilted; polyester batting, signed & dated. $196.00

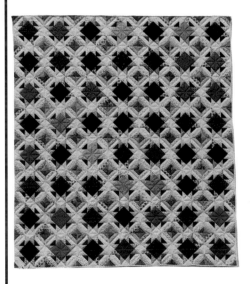

410989 – CENTER: CONTENTMENT; 72" x 80"; poly/cotton; made in Kentucky in 1989; machine & hand embroidered top, hand quilted. $259.00

510989 – CENTER RIGHT: NITE AND NOON; 84½" x 104"; multi-colors with white; cotton & polyester; made in 1987; hand pieced, hand quilted; polyester batting. $575.00

610989 – BOTTOM LEFT: LOG CABIN; 80" x 106"; lightcolors; cotton/polyester; made in Missouri in 1988; machine pieced, hand quilted; polyester batting. $345.00

710989 – BOTTOM RIGHT: OLD FASHIONED GIRL; 90" x 100"; deep rose, black, white; cotton; made in Pennsylvania in 1988; hand embroidery, hand quilted; Fairfield batting. $460.00

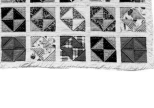

111989 – TOP LEFT: CHECKER-BOARDS; 92" x 92"; browns, orange, pink, green; cotton; made c. 1870; hand & machine pieced, hand quilted; colors still bright, 3 small holes, some age stains on back, initials WAC embroidered on border. $690.00

211989 – TOP RIGHT: OLD MAID'S PUZZLE; 65" x 93"; multi-color; cotton & blend; top made in Kentucky in 1932 & quilted in 1986; hand pieced & quilted; tiny stitches, Hi-Loft Poly batting. $299.00

311989 – CENTER LEFT: LOG CABIN; 42" x 54"; pinks & blues; cottons & blends; made in Mississippi in 1987; machine pieced, hand quilted; sawtooth edging, polyester batting. $69.00

411989 – CENTER: TREE OF LIFE; 84"

x 102"; greens, blues, brown, tan, yellow, oranges, dark brown; all cotton; made in Missouri in 1988; cross-stitched, hand quilted; pointed edge trim. $460.00

511989 – CENTER RIGHT: JEWISH STAR; 86" x 102"; white, yellow & brown; polyester & cotton; made in Illinois in 1987; hand embroidered & quilted; small print calicos. $345.00

611989 – BOTTOM LEFT: GRAND-MOTHER'S FAN; 76" x 87"; mauve & slate blue calico & solid; cotton; made in Georgia in 1989; hand pieced, hand quilted; border is white polyester, white backing. $460.00

711989 – BOTTOM RIGHT: NINE PATCH; 87" x 105"; navy print; cotton/-poly; made in New Jersey in 1988; machine pieced, hand quilted. $403.00

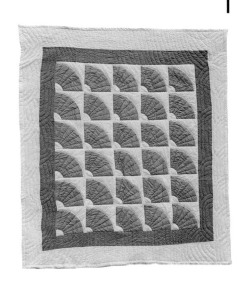

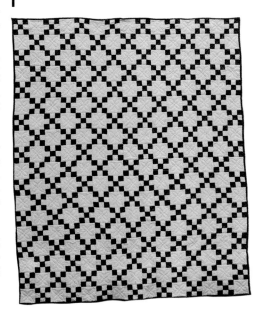

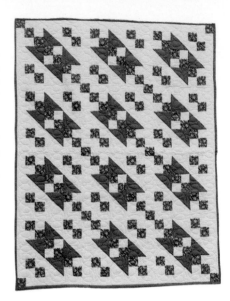

112989 – TOP LEFT: COLORADO LOG CABIN; 89" x 101"; blue; cotton/polyester; made in Missouri in 1989; machine pieced, hand quilted; polyester batting. $403.00

212989 – TOP RIGHT: JACOB'S LADDER; 72" x 94"; mauve & white; cotton & poly blends; made in Illinois in 1986; machine pieced, machine quilted; lining is white, bonded poly batting. $173.00

312989 – CENTER LEFT: ALBUM BLOCK; 71" x 88"; red, white & blue; 1940's calico; made in Arkansas c. 1940; hand pieced, hand quilted; 5 st./in., primitive quilting. $230.00

412989 – CENTER: PIECED HEART; 69" x 91"; pinks, blues & white; cotton;

made in New York in 1989; hand appliqued, machine pieced & quilted; polyester batting. $244.00

512989 – CENTER RIGHT: LOG CABIN; 93" x 108"; pink, rose & cranberry; cotton polyester; made in Illinois; machine pieced, hand quilted. $230.00

612989 – BOTTOM LEFT: BUDDING STAR; 92" x 96"; multi-color; cotton/polyester; made in Missouri in 1989; machine pieced, hand quilted; cream background, polyester batting. $374.00

712989 – BOTTOM RIGHT: STRING QUILT; 72" x 82"; mixed solids & prints; cotton; made in Kentucky in 1935; hand pieced, hand quilted; primitive. $259.00

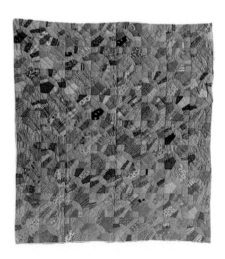

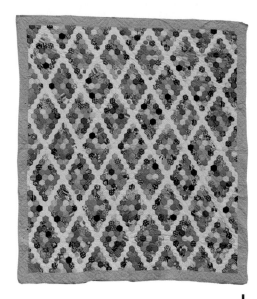

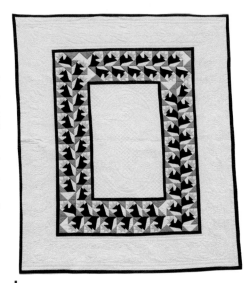

113989 – TOP LEFT: HEXAGON FLOWER GARDEN; 88" x 102"; multi-color on white; cotton; made in Illinois c. 1930; machine pieced, hand quilted; all cotton batting. $575.00

213989 – TOP RIGHT: MOUNTAIN LILY; 78½" x 93½"; white, green & yellow; cotton; made in California in 1985; machine pieced, hand quilted; pre-shrunk. $460.00

313989 – CENTER LEFT: GRAND-MOTHER'S FLOWER GARDEN; 76" x 94"; prints & melon; cotton & poly blends; made in Kentucky in 1985; hand pieced, hand quilted. $201.00

413989 – CENTER: BOW TIE; 78" x 60"; multi-color; cotton; made in

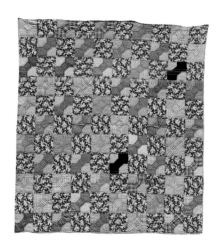

Tennessee in 1935; hand pieced, hand quilted; 7" blocks. $190.00

513989 – CENTER RIGHT: CRAZY PATCH; 78" x 87"; multi-color/embroidery; cotton, silks, velvets; made in Illinois c. 1880's; hand pieced, hand quilted; some silks frayed. $920.00

613989 – BOTTOM LEFT: PURPLE PASSION; 96" x 117"; shades of purple; cotton & polyester; made in 1985; cross stitched, machine pieced, hand quilted. $518.00

713989 – BOTTOM RIGHT: TURKEY TRACKS; 73" x 94"; multi-color; cotton & cotton/poly; hand quilted in Missouri in 1989; top machine pieced c. 1945, Dacron batting. $161.00

114989 – TOP LEFT: BLAZING STAR; 76" x 88"; red & blue; polyester & cotton; made in Tennessee in 1989; hand pieced, hand quilted; bonded polyester batting. $345.00

214989 – TOP RIGHT: DAHLIA; 87" x 104"; lavender/purple/gold accent; cotton/poly; made in Oregon in 1988; machine pieced, hand quilted; polyester batting, double bias binding. $259.00

314989 – CENTER LEFT: FLYING SWALLOW; 95" x 99"; blue; cotton/polyester; made in Missouri in 1989; machine pieced, hand quilted; polyester batting. $345.00

414989 – CENTER: STRING BLOCK; 76½" x 64"; multi; cotton; made in Kentucky in 1935; hand pieced & quilt-

ed; primitive, few nicks on hem. $288.00

514989 – CENTER RIGHT: PROGRESSIVE FARMER ANNIVERSARY QUILT; 82" x 98"; blue, gold & maroon; cotton-polyester; made in Arkansas in 1987; hand appliqued & quilted; pieced border, polyester batting. $575.00

614989 – BOTTOM LEFT: ALPHABET & NUMBERS; 46" x 46"; pastel solids & ginghams; cotton poly; made in Missouri in 1988; machine pieced, hand tied; solids have a letter or number embroidered. $63.00

714989 – BOTTOM RIGHT: SUMMER QUIETUDE; 92" x 101"; blue & mauve; cotton; made in Oregon in 1989; machine pieced & quilted; Mountain Mist fat batting. $385.00

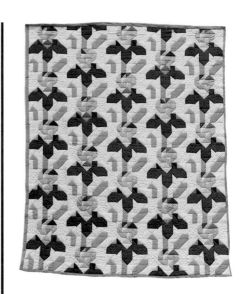

115989 – TOP LEFT: BROWN APPLI-QUE; 81" x 96"; brown & white; cotton; made in Illinois in 1989; machine pieced, hand quilted. $345.00

215989 – TOP RIGHT: IRIS; 71" x 85"; purple, lavender prints & assorted colors; broadcloth, cottons; made in Tennessee in 1988; hand pieced, hand quilted; polyester batting. $345.00

315989 – CENTER LEFT: MY WILD AMISH CHAIN; 70" x 83"; gray, pink, mauve & black; cotton & poly cotton; made in North Dakota in 1989; machine pieced, hand & machine quilted; signed & dated. $299.00

415989 – CENTER: STRING STAR QUILT; 104" x 104"; multi-color with

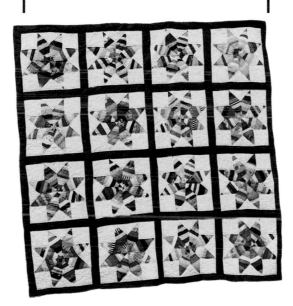

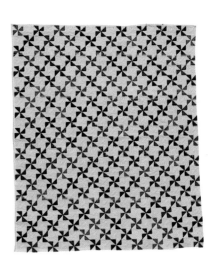

brown; polyester, cotton; made in 1980; machine pieced, hand quilted. $345.00

515989 – CENTER RIGHT: PINWHEEL; 70¾" x 84"; white, red, blue, brown, black & maroon; 75% cotton, 25% blends; made in Idaho in 1989; machine pieced, hand quilted; unbleached muslin. $431.00

615989 – BOTTOM LEFT: FLORAL ARRAY; 90" x 108"; soft blue; cotton/poly blend; made in Ohio in 1988; hand quilted; thick polyester batting. $410.00

715989 – BOTTOM RIGHT: FLOWER BASKETS; 82" x 99"; red & white; cotton; made in Wisconsin in 1989; machine pieced, hand quilted. $520.00

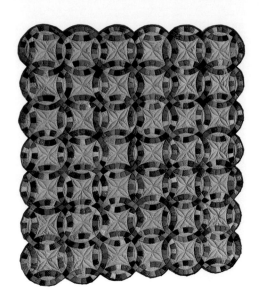

116989 – TOP LEFT: LONE STAR; 42" x 42"; forest green & off-white; cotton & polyester/cotton; made in Missouri in 1989; machine pieced, hand quilted; made by Mennonites, some stains. $115.00

216989 – TOP RIGHT: DOUBLE WEDDING RING; 88" x 98"; multi-color; cotton; made in Tennessee in 1988; machine pieced, hand quilted; beige background, brown binding. $374.00

316989 – CENTER LEFT: ALBUM; 67½" x 75"; mixed colors; cotton blends; made in Tennessee in 1955; hand pieced & quilted; muslin background, lightweight. $155.00

416989 – CENTER: GIANT DAHLIA; 103" x 110"; yellow & brown; 100% cot-

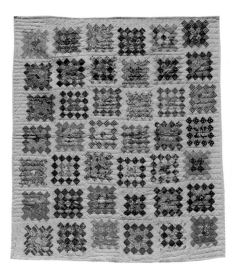

ton; made in Colorado in 1985; machine pieced, hand quilted; signed & dated, pre-washed. $546.00

516989 – CENTER RIGHT: TRIP AROUND THE WORLD; 35" x 35"; reds & greens; cotton; made in Georgia in 1987; machine pieced, hand quilted. $115.00

616989 – BOTTOM LEFT: FEATHERED STAR; 34" x 34"; white, yellow & pink; cotton; made in 1970; hand quilted; small stain. $144.00

716989 – BOTTOM RIGHT: TUMBLIN' STAR; 96" x 100"; blue & rust; cotton & cotton blends; made in Alabama in 1981; machine & hand quilted; sheet lining. $345.00

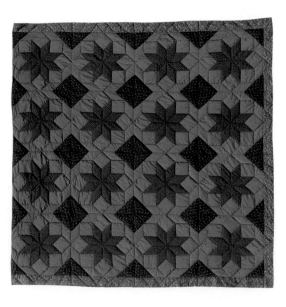

117989 – TOP LEFT: CAJUN MINIATURE CHRISTMAS QUILT; 25½" x 25½"; brick red, dark green; cotton & cotton blends; made in Louisiana in 1989; machine pieced, hand quilted; stars are quilted along off-white background. $115.00

217989 – TOP RIGHT: CHRISTMAS SNOWFLAKES; 42" x 42"; red, green & white; cotton/poly blends; made in Oregon in 1989; machine pieced & quilted in-the-ditch, hand quilted snowflakes in 20 white boxes, polyester batting. $138.00

317989 – CENTER LEFT: CHRISTMAS LONE STAR; 36" x 36"; reds & greens; cotton, cotton/polyester; made in Minnesota in 1989; hand pieced, hand quilted; feathered hearts quilted in large open areas, polyester batting. $115.00

417989 – CENTER: GIANT DAHLIA; 62" round; reds & greens; cotton; made

in Florida in 1986; machine pieced, hand quilted; Christmas prints, backed in white cotton, Mountain Mist batting. $288.00

517989 – CENTER RIGHT: CHRISTMAS STAR; 35" x 35"; white, reds & greens; cotton/polyester blends; made in Kentucky in 1989; machine pieced, hand quilted; Christmas prints, polyester fiber-fil batting. $190.00

617989 – BOTTOM LEFT: DRUNKARD'S PATH; 82" x 100"; rose, off-white, brown print; percale & muslin; made in Kentucky in 1988; hand pieced, hand quilted; polyester batting. $403.00

717989 – BOTTOM RIGHT: CHRISTMAS TREE; 37" x 37"; reds, greens, white; cotton/cotton blends; made in California in 1989; machine pieced, hand quilted; Log Cabin tree of varied Christmas calicos. $98.00

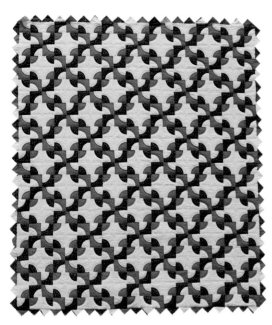

118989 – TOP LEFT: PROSPERITY STAR; 70" x 82"; yellow, blue, pink & red; cotton; made in Pennsylvania in 1940; hand pieced, hand quilted; cotton batting. $345.00

218989 – TOP RIGHT: AMISH NINE PATCH; 34½" x 34½"; dark Amish shades with dark blue predominating; 100% cotton; made in New Hampshire 1989; machine pieced, hand appliqued; dogwood blossom design in each dark blue square, pre-washed. $115.00

318989 – CENTER LEFT: FINE FEATHERED STAR; 50½" x 50½"; blue, mauve; cotton; made in Kentucky in 1989; machine pieced, hand quilted; pre-washed, muslin backing, 100% polyester batting, signed & dated. $230.00

418989 – CENTER: PROBABLY PISTACHIO; 24" x 39"; oranges, yellows,

pinks, melons, green; satin, taffeta, linen, cotton, cotton/poly; made in Wisconsin in 1988; machine pieced, hand appliqued & quilted; light green background. $151.00

518989 – CENTER RIGHT: TRIP A-ROUND THE WORLD; 38" x 49"; tan, blue & red; cotton; made in Vermont in 1987; machine pieced, tied; cotton/-polyester backing. $60.00

618989 – BOTTOM LEFT: LOG CABIN; 24" x 24"; pink & green; 100% cotton; made in Texas in 1989; machine pieced, hand quilted; heart quilting in border. $115.00

718989 – BOTTOM RIGHT: TRIP AROUND THE WORLD; 37" x 43"; multi-colored; cotton; made in Indiana in 1988; machine pieced, hand quilted; mint green backing, polyester batting. $86.00

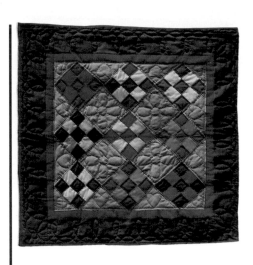

119989 – TOP LEFT: A SAMPLER QUILT; 45" x 45"; peach, brown & greens; 100% cotton; made in Connecticut; machine pieced, hand quilted & appliqued; features hand embroidery with hand finished binding, bears are trapuntoed into picture frame, polyester batting. $201.00

219989 – TOP RIGHT: 9 PATCH; 29" x 29"; blues, reds, lavender; cotton blend; made in Pennsylvania; machine pieced, hand quilted; made by Amish grandmother from her scraps. $98.00

319989 – CENTER LEFT: EMBROIDERED CRIB QUILT; 42" x 64"; red & white; cotton; made in 1940; machine pieced, hand quilted; red embroidery, 40 blocks with designs of children, animals, flowers & fruits. $445.00

419989 – CENTER: CIRCUS ELEPHANT; 26" x 35"; gold, dark red; cot-

ton/cotton blends; made in Wisconsin in 1988; machine pieced, hand quilted; adaptation of doll quilt. $92.00

519989 – CENTER RIGHT: MOON OVER THE MOUNTAIN; 85" x 52"; assorted colors; cotton & polyester; made in Tennessee in 1976; machine pieced, hand quilted; yellow moon over each mountain, light blue lining. $144.00

619989 – BOTTOM LEFT: PASTEL WINDMILL; 32" x 38"; soft blue, pink, lilac, green & cream; cotton; made in Connecticut; machine pieced, hand quilted; combination of Star & Windmill patterns, 5" cream border quilted with ostrich plume quilting. $115.00

719989 – BOTTOM RIGHT: TRIANGLE STAR; 43" x 43"; reds & greens; cottons & cotton blends; made in Utah in 1988; machine pieced, hand quilted; new prewashed fabrics, over 2,000 triangles. $60.00

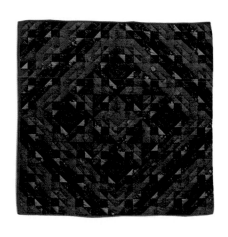

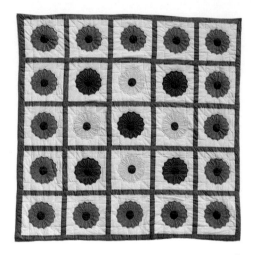

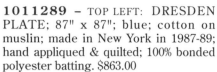

1011289 – TOP LEFT: DRESDEN PLATE; 87" x 87"; blue; cotton on muslin; made in New York in 1987-89; hand appliqued & quilted; 100% bonded polyester batting. $863.00

2011289 – TOP RIGHT: LOG CABIN; 71" x 84"; assorted colors; cotton & cotton blends; made in Arkansas in 1988; machine pieced, hand quilted. $230.00

3011289 – CENTER LEFT: WIND-BLOWN TULIPS; 82" x 102"; pastels – blue, green, rose, off-white; cotton; made in 1989; hand appliqued & quilted; alternate plain blocks quilted in a "wind-blown" effect, borders have patterns of flowers, leaves & marching scallops, hand bound with double fabric. $500.00

4011289 – CENTER: STAR GARDEN; 90" x 90"; blues & reds, off-white background; 100% cotton; made in Massachusetts in 1988; machine pieced, hand appliqued & quilted; Hobbs polyester batting, blue ribbon winner. $1,380.00

5011289 – CENTER RIGHT: POTTED STAR FLOWER; 21" x 36"; red, green, white; cotton, cotton/polyester; made in Minnesota in 1989; hand pieced & quilted; flower & vine motif quilted in large white spaces, sleeve on back. $115.00

6011289 – BOTTOM LEFT: LITTLE GIRL'S DELIGHT; 57" x 82"; pink, mint green & white; 100% cotton & poly/cotton; made in Illinois in 1988; machine pieced, hand quilted; bunnies, geese & Mrs. Mouse are busy in scenes of this nursery rhyme inspired quilt, printed panel with coordinating borders added, hand sewn binding. $110.00

7011289 – BOTTOM RIGHT: VARIATION GRANDMOTHER'S OWN I; 70" x 78"; teal paisley print, burgundy & white; 100% cotton broadcloth/polished cotton; made in Michigan in 1988; machine pieced, hand quilted. $190.00

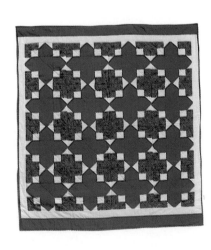

1031289 – TOP LEFT: BARN RAISING LOG CABIN; 88" x 95"; royal blue & white; poly cotton blends; made in Illinois in 1988; machine pieced, machine quilted; white lining with bonded poly batting, binding is double fabric & double stitched. $207.00

2031289 – TOP RIGHT: VARIABLE SQUARES; 72" x 76"; burgundy with blue & black; 100% cotton plaids, gingham & prints; made in 1900; hand pieced, hand quilted; slight wearing spot in center of backing where folded. $460.00

3031289 – CENTER LEFT: LONE STAR; 80" x 92"; multi-colored prints in star with beige & green border; cotton; made in Montana in 1987; hand pieced, hand quilted; patterns of fabric in star are color coordinated. $345.00

4031289 – CENTER: CANIS SOUTHERN CALIFORNIUS (Wild Doggies); 43" x 43"; brights on white; cotton & cotton blends; made in California in 1988;

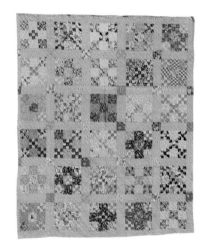

machine pieced, hand quilted; sturdy for everyday use, polyester batting, hanging sleeve, signed & dated. $345.00

5031289 – CENTER RIGHT: NINE PATCH; 68" x 85"; multi-color with yellow, red & blue prints; cotton; made in Kansas in 1930's; machine pieced, hand quilted; thin cotton batting, very light weight, backing is yellow print cotton. $230.00

6031289 – BOTTOM LEFT: CAKESTAND; 64" x 79"; subtle Amish tones of black, tan, gold, teal, mauve, blue solids; 100% cottons; made in Iowa in 1988; machine pieced, hand quilted; ticking stripe print backing, poly low-loft batting, black quilting thread, never used. $253.00

7031289 – BOTTOM RIGHT: FORGET-ME-NOTS; 84" x 100"; blue & green on beige background; cotton-polyester blends; made in Ohio in 1988; hand quilted, hand appliqued. $575.00

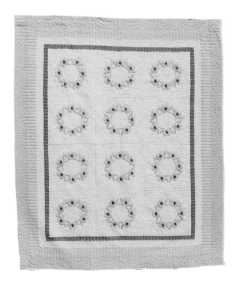

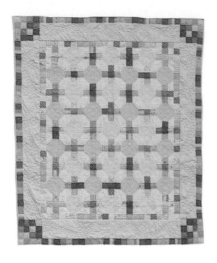

1041289 – TOP LEFT: SNOWBALL PUZZLE; 75" x 88"; pink, blue & lavender; cotton & cotton blends; made in North Dakota in 1989; machine pieced & quilted; quilted with double heart flowers in snowballs & a heart vine & heart flower pattern on borders, signed & dated. $276.00

2041289 – TOP RIGHT: DUTCHMAN PUZZLE; 83" x 99"; rose pink with black print & beige; cotton & cotton blends; made in Arkansas in 1988; machine pieced, hand quilted; double binding, polyester batting. $230.00

3041289 – CENTER LEFT: AUNT SUKEY'S CHOICE; 75" x 89"; scrap quilt with green border; cotton & cotton blends; made in Washington in 1977; machine pieced, hand quilted; polyester batting. $345.00

4041289 – CENTER: SUNBONNET SUE & FARMER BILL; 43" x 51"; green

& white with multi-colors; cotton/poly; made in Illinois in 1989; hand appliqued, machine pieced, hand quilted. $87.00

5041289 – CENTER RIGHT: COLONIAL GARDEN; 76" x 96"; pinks, green & burgundy on white; cotton; made in Indiana in 1987; hand appliqued, hand quilted; made from kit, never used. $662.00

6041289 – BOTTOM LEFT: LOG CABIN STAR; 88" x 102"; shades of blue with touch of pink; all cotton; made in Kansas in 1989; machine pieced, hand quilted; poly filled batting with poly cotton backing, has double binding with mitered corners. $460.00

7041289 – BOTTOM RIGHT: SUGAR LOAF; 82" x 92"; combination of prints; cotton; made in Missouri in 1975; machine pieced, hand quilted; narrow border of small blue flower, 9-patch block in 4 corners, 8 st./1". $460.00

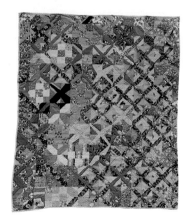

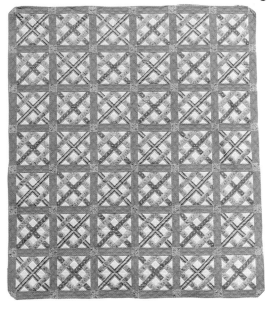

1061289 – TOP LEFT: STRING; 68" x 80"; mixed; cotton; made in Tennessee in 1930; hand pieced, hand quilted; 30's fabrics are very evident. $144.00

2061289 – TOP RIGHT: KENTUCKY CHAIN; 90" x 104"; rose & green; cotton & cotton/poly; machine pieced, machine quilted; hand finished. $345.00

3061289 – CENTER LEFT: "NA PUA O HAWAII"; 46" x 69"; red, brown, coral, tan, green & pink; 100% cotton; made in Hawaii in 1989; hand pieced, hand quilted; new quilt, flowers of Hawaii. $690.00

4061289 – CENTER: 3 BASKETS; 27½" x 51"; cranberry paisley with navy & tans; cotton; made in Wisconsin in 1989; machine pieced, hand quilted; hanging sleeve. $75.00

5061289 – CENTER RIGHT: DELECTABLE MOUNTAIN WILD FLOWER; 40" x 40"; tones of blue with brown/gold; cotton/poly; made in Illinois in 1988; hand appliqued, machine pieced, hand quilted; wallhanging with yo-yo flowers hand appliqued. $288.00

6061289 – BOTTOM LEFT: BOW TIE; 94" x 70"; prints on muslin; cotton & cotton blends; made in Kentucky; hand pieced in 1934, hand quilted in 1988; hi-loft poly batting, old fashioned quilting. $299.00

7061289 – BOTTOM RIGHT: DRESDEN PLATE; 87" x 104"; slate blue & rose; all cotton; made in Kansas in 1988; machine pieced, hand appliqued, hand quilted; Mountain Mist batting, mitered corners, signed & dated, never used. $449.00

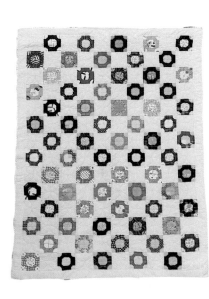

1071289 – TOP LEFT: JACOB'S LAD-DER; 66" x 94"; natural, green & orange; 100% cotton; made in Louisiana in 1989; machine pieced, hand quilted; poly batting. $288.00

2071289 – TOP RIGHT: MARTHA WASHINGTON FLOWER GARDEN; 72" x 94¼"; mixed; cotton; made in Kentucky in 1935; hand pieced, hand quilted; very colorful, solids & prints drawn together by green diamonds, scalloped edges. $345.00

3071289 – CENTER LEFT: ROAD TO CALIFORNIA; 84" x 98"; brown, red & camel; poly/cotton; made in Ohio in 1983; machine pieced, hand quilted; polyester batting. $460.00

4071289 – CENTER: HOME IS WHERE THE HEART IS; 41" x 41"; blue/ecru; 100% cotton; made in New Hampshire in 1988; machine pieced,

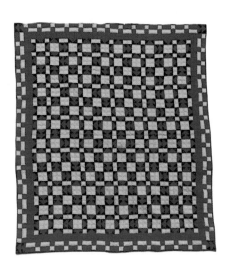

hand quilted; 100% polyester low loft batting, traditional house block alternating with plain block, quilted in intricate feathered heart design. $161.00

5071289 – CENTER RIGHT: OHIO STAR; 83" x 98"; multi-color; cotton; made in Kentucky; hand pieced, hand quilted. $345.00

6071289 – BOTTOM LEFT: FLOWER BASKET; 90" x 90"; brown, off-white & multi-color; cotton; made in Illinois in 1988; hand pieced, hand quilted. $455.00

7071289 – BOTTOM RIGHT: DRESDEN PLATE; 90" x 106"; dark mauve & assorted pieces; cotton & poly blends; made in Kansas in 1989; machine pieced, hand quilted, hand appliqued; background pieces are dark mauve, stripping a small print, sheet lining. $374.00

1081289 – TOP LEFT: ALTERNATING BLOCK PATTERN; 77" x 96"; red, hunter green, gold & plaid; top is wool blend & back is cotton flannel; made in Ohio in 1989; machine pieced, tied. $288.00

2081289 – TOP RIGHT: LOG CABIN; 76" x 88"; tan to brown; all cotton; made in Alabama in 1989; hand quilted; double quilted, sheet lining, poly batting. $288.00

3081289 – CENTER LEFT: GOLDEN ANNIVERSARY HEART PATTERN; 77½" x 91½"; gold & white; poly-blend cottons; made in Texas in 1985; machine pieced, hand tied; center square has embroidery & gold fabric paint with words "Golden Wedding Anniversary – 50th" within heart, love birds, double rings & bells, center is "framed" with white lace over gold fabric, buyer can add names & dates in the center if desired, fabric paint or embroidery can be used to sign guest or family names in the blocks. $156.00

4081289 – CENTER: WEATHERVANE;

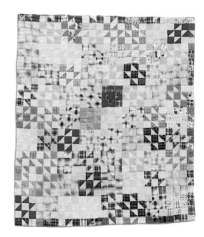

36" x 36"; burgundy, tan, rose; 100% cotton; made in Connecticut in 1988; machine pieced, hand quilted; solid fabrics are polished cotton, tan print has burgundy & rose flowers to coordinate with solid fabrics, each shape in weather vane is hand quilted in cream thread so that quilting shows. $115.00

5081289 – CENTER RIGHT: CONTRARY WIFE; 75" x 84½"; mixed; cotton; made in Tennessee in 1945; hand pieced, hand quilted, varied colors, assorted checks, stripes, solids & prints, primitive handwork. $115.00

6081289 – BOTTOM LEFT: STEPS TO THE GARDEN; 78" x 102"; white, red & assorted; cotton & polyester; made in Illinois in 1988; machine pieced, hand quilted. $322.00

7081289 – BOTTOM RIGHT: OHIO STAR; 90" x 108"; pastels on white; cotton; made in Kentucky in 1988; cotton batting. $403.00

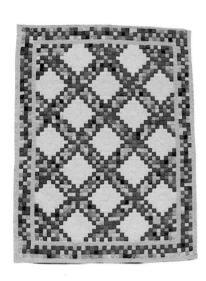

1101289 – TOP LEFT: ROYAL STAR OF MISSISSIPPI; 89" x 95"; rust & brown; cotton polyester; made in Missouri in 1988; machine pieced, hand quilted; prints & solids, cream fill polyester batting. $345.00

2101289 – TOP RIGHT: PINWHEEL; 83" x 90"; brown, white & yellow; cotton & polyester; made in Illinois in 1988; hand embroidered, hand quilted; white muslin & printed calico, pinwheel is brown & inside yellow flowers, calico is small brown print. $322.00

3101289 – CENTER LEFT: WHIG ROSE; 80" x 80"; red, green, pink, yellow & ivory; cotton; made in Pennyslvania in 1880; hand quilted, hand appliqued; traditional pattern was handmade. $1,265.00

4101289 – CENTER: DOUBLE WEDDING RING; 42" x 42"; multi-color; cotton/polyester; made in Missouri in 1989;

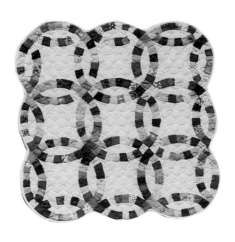

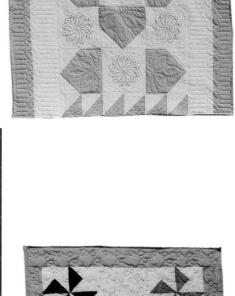

machine pieced, machine quilted; white fill, polyester batting. $41.00

5101289 – CENTER RIGHT: PINWHEEL; 43" x 43"; yellow & green; cotton/polyester; made in Missouri in 1989; machine pieced, machine quilted; made of green prints with cream & white, set together with yellow print blocks. $46.00

6101289 – BOTTOM LEFT: ROYAL STAR OF NEVADA; 85" x 95"; rust, brown & peach; cotton polyester; made in Missouri in 1989; machine pieced, hand quilted; star is made of 16 diamonds. $345.00

7101289 – BOTTOM RIGHT: CROSS-STITCH TULIPS; 78" x 93"; blues, lavender & white; cotton & cotton blends; made in Minnesota in 1984; machine pieced, hand quilted; cross-stitched squares are from a kit, 24 tulip blocks & a scalloped border on 3 sides, tulip design quilted in sash & border. $499.00

1111289 – TOP LEFT: FEATHERED STARS; 89" x 108"; reds, med. blue & cream; 100% cotton, pre-washed; made in Virginia in 1985; machine pieced, hand quilted, hand appliqued border; Ultra loft poly bonded batting, muslin backing, double binding. $460.00

2111289 – TOP RIGHT: GRAND-MOTHER'S FAN; 89" x 89"; multi-pastel/cream; cotton; made in Wisconsin in 1988; machine pieced, hand quilted; fine feathering, fits flat on bed without pillow tuck. $575.00

3111289 – CENTER LEFT: TREE OF LIFE; 78" x 94"; bright blue, red, orange, yellow & green; percale & cotton blends; made in Indiana in 1988; hand made; polyester batting, winner at Posey County Fair. $1,150.00

4111289 – CENTER: MINIATURE TULIP; 22" x 29"; pink & melon; cotton/poly; made in Illinois in 1988; machine pieced, hand quilted; beautiful doll quilt or wallhanging. $64.00

5111289 – CENTER RIGHT: G.W.T.W. – THE MOVIE; 82" x 82"; various movie scenes; cottons, poly, cotton blends, velvet, etc; made in Minnesota in 1989; hand pieced, appliqued & quilted. $1,725.00

6111289 – BOTTOM LEFT: PRINCESS FEATHER; 84" x 89"; deep rose, med. blue & white; cotton & cotton blend; made in Missouri in 1982; hand pieced, hand quilted, hand appliqued; applique done with buttonhole stitch, quilted with thread to match colors, polyester batting, pattern from a 90-year-old quilt, very bright & cheerful, never used. $460.00

7111289 – BOTTOM RIGHT: MIRROR IMAGE FAN; 86" x 96"; rainbow colors; cotton/polyester; made in Missouri in 1988; machine pieced, hand quilted; each fan is same, polyester batting. $345.00

1121289 – TOP LEFT: LONE STAR QUILT; 98" x 110"; emerald green & dusty rose; cotton & polyester/cotton; made in Missouri in 1989; machine pieced, hand quilted; quilted by Mennonites. $448.00

2121289 – TOP RIGHT: FLYING GEESE; 58" x 72"; pink geese on scraps with green sashing strips; cotton; top made late 1800's, quilted in New York in 1989; hand & machine pieced, hand quilted; few patches may have been replaced by later fabrics, heavily quilted, cotton classic batting. $345.00

3121289 – CENTER LEFT: MONKEY WRENCH; 82" x 101"; apricot with avacado & rose print; cotton & cotton polyester; made in Indiana in 1987; machine pieced, hand quilted; polyester batting, pre-washed. $460.00

4121289 – CENTER: SOUTHERN STAR; 43" x 43"; pink & blue; 100% cotton; made in Louisiana in 1989; machine pieced, hand quilted, hand appliqued; pink & blue prints on solid pink background, original tulip pattern, solid pink backing. $173.00

5121289 – CENTER RIGHT: EMBROIDERED STAR; 87" x 100"; lilac & purple; cotton & poly; made in Illinois in 1989; hand embroidered, hand quilted; embroidered with shades of lilac, purple & light green, bound in prairie point & is reversible. $288.00

6121289 – BOTTOM LEFT: CALICO DAISY; 80" x 96"; white & yellow calico; cotton; made in Illinois in 1988. $575.00

7121289 – BOTTOM RIGHT: SOUTHERN BELLE; 86" x 94"; multi-color, light blue & white; cotton & cotton blends; made in Alabama in 1989; hand quilted, hand appliqued; cotton batting. $345.00

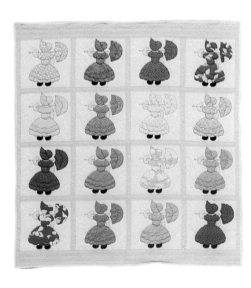

1131289 – TOP LEFT: LONE STAR; 90" x 102"; rose shades to pink & wine, ecru; cotton & cotton/polyester; made in Indiana in 1989; machine pieced, hand quilted; printed border, ecru background, polyester batting, made by Mennonites. $426.00

2131289 – TOP RIGHT: LOG CABIN; 84" x 108"; varied; cotton & cotton polyester; made in Arkansas in 1989; machine pieced, hand quilted. $259.00

3131289 – CENTER LEFT: CAT'S CRADLE; 45" x 45"; black, white with gray, maroon & red squares; blocks unknown & rest 100% cotton; made in Mississippi; hand pieced & quilted; blocks were pieced about 1930 & washed, quilted by hand in 1989. $179.00

4131289 – CENTER: MARTHA WASHINGTON FLOWER GARDEN; 100" x 102"; light to dark; all cotton; made in

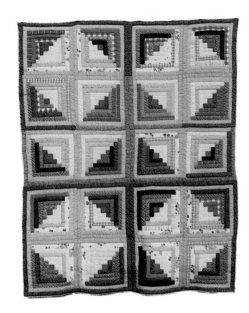

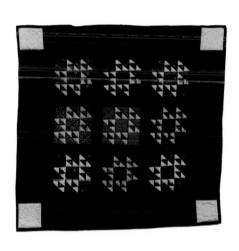

Alabama in 1987; hand quilted; pre-washed fabric, sheet lining, quilting on each side of seam. $518.00

5131289 – CENTER RIGHT: ENTHUSIASM; 24" x 31½"; turquoise, fuchsia, white; cotton; made in Connecticut in 1988; machine pieced, hand quilted; original design, machine pieced then hand appliqued onto background. $98.00

6131289 – BOTTOM LEFT: BOSTON COMMONS; 106" x 110"; dusty rose; cotton & polyester & polyester; made in Missouri in 1989; machine pieced, hand quilted; feather quilting with sawtooth edging, Mennonite quilted. $748.00

7131289 – BOTTOM RIGHT: TIED CRIB QUILT; 42" x 51"; blue & white; poly-cotton blend; made in Mississippi in 1988; machine pieced, hand tied with yarn; crib quilt or wallhanging, Polyfil 100% polyester batting. $41.00

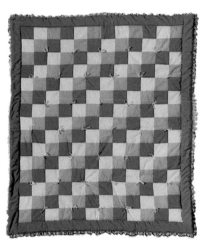

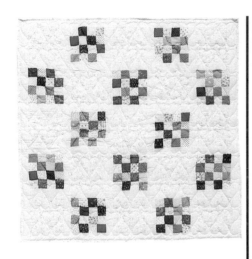

1151289 – TOP LEFT: PATCHWORK; 51" x 51"; multi-color with yellow setting; cotton/polyester; made in Missouri in 1989; machine pieced, machine quilted; polyester batting. $52.00

2151289 – TOP RIGHT: AIGYPTOS; 63" x 80"; desert sand, black, turquoise & jewel tones; cotton, polished cotton; made in 1988; Mountain Mist batting, black borders are quilted in white showing hippos, fish & lotus; applique shows market scene, 2 women silhouettes appliqued on back. $1,725.00

3151289 – CENTER LEFT: JACOB'S LADDER; 69" x 72"; red, blue, white, small amounts of green, brown & black; cotton; made in North Carolina in 1930-40; machine pieced, hand quilted; very thin. $460.00

4151289 – CENTER: LA'A ULU – Spring-Time of Growth; 40" x 54"; yellow & white; Imperial Broadcloth, 50/50

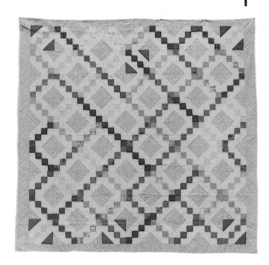

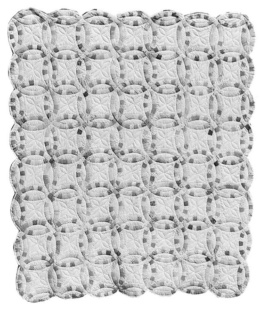

poly/cotton; made in Marshall Islands in 1989; hand quilted, hand appliqued; quilting ½" apart, tulip design in border areas, machine washable. $322.00

5151289 – CENTER RIGHT: LOG CABIN; 89" x 109"; maroon, navy, ecru; polyester/cotton; made in Ohio in 1988; machine pieced, hand quilted; polyester batting. $391.00

6151289 – BOTTOM LEFT: DOUBLE WEDDING RING; 90" x 105"; multi-color; cotton/polyester; made in Missouri in 1989; machine pieced, hand quilted; cream background, cotton/polyester batting. $345.00

7151289 – BOTTOM RIGHT: KALEIDO-SCOPE; 42" x 52"; multi-prints & muslin; 100% cotton & poly-cotton; made in Illinois in 1989; machine pieced, hand quilted; signed & dated. $202.00

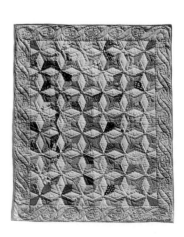

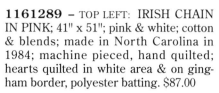

1161289 – TOP LEFT: IRISH CHAIN IN PINK; 41" x 51"; pink & white; cotton & blends; made in North Carolina in 1984; machine pieced, hand quilted; hearts quilted in white area & on gingham border, polyester batting. $87.00

2161289 – TOP RIGHT: LONE STAR; 102" x 102"; rust, black, green, brown on stone colored background; cottons; made in Missouri in 1984; hand pieced, quilted & appliqued; flowers are original design by Mary Sorenson. $1,582.00

3161289 – CENTER LEFT: CUP & SAUCER; 77" x 92"; assorted; knit; made in Kentucky in 1985; machine pieced, hand quilted; knit lining. $115.00

4161289 – CENTER: BLUE STARS OVER FLYING GEESE; 30" x 47"; navy, blues & tan; cotton; made in Wisconsin

in 1989; machine pieced, hand quilted; sleeved & signed. $115.00

5161289 – CENTER RIGHT: LOKELANI – ROSE OF HEAVEN; 33" x 33"; pink & dusty rose; Imperial Broadcloth, 50/50 poly/cotton, 100% cotton; made in Marshall Islands in 1989; hand quilted, hand appliqued; echo quilting with ½" between rows. $202.00

6161289 – BOTTOM LEFT: FLYING GEESE; 86" x 101"; shades of blue, rose, green with yellow; cotton/cotton polyester; made in Indiana in 1986; machine pieced; Mennonite quilter, prewashed, polyester batting. $529.00

7161289 – BOTTOM RIGHT: DOUBLE WEDDING RING; 83" x 107"; blue; cotton/polyester; made in Missouri in 1989; machine pieced, hand quilted; polyester batting, white fill. $345.00

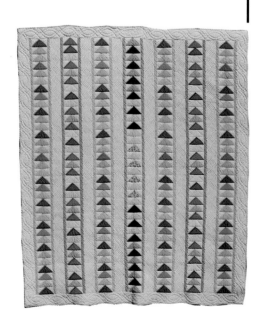

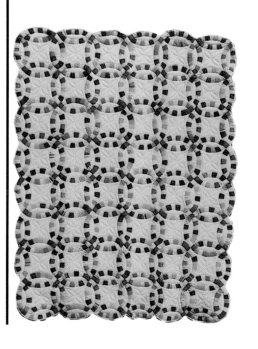

1171289 – TOP LEFT: LOG CABIN; 98" x 116"; browns & pinks; polyester; made in Illinois in 1989; hand quilted. $230.00

2171289 – TOP RIGHT: DOUBLE IRISH CHAIN; 33" x 43"; cream & green; cotton; made in Indiana in 1989; machine pieced, hand quilted; polyester batting, cream background with blue hearts & pink & green flowers. $58.00

3171289 – CENTER LEFT: DOUBLE WEDDING RING; 80" x 109"; multi-color with light yellow background; cotton/polyester; made in Missouri in 1989; machine pieced, hand quilted; polyester batting. $345.00

4171289 – CENTER: DOUBLE NINE-PATCH; 38" x 38"; multi-color with

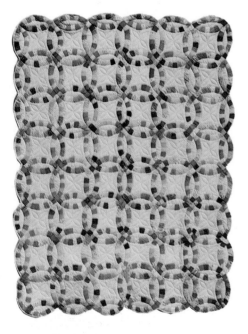

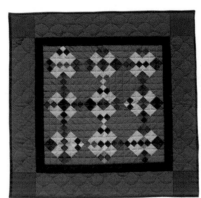

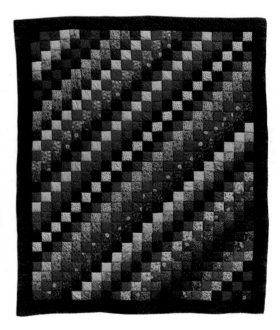

mauve & purple predominant; 100% cotton; made in Georgia in 1987; machine pieced, hand quilted; traditional Amish design. $115.00

5171289 – CENTER RIGHT: STREAK OF LIGHTNING; 92" x 108"; browns, golds & rusts; cotton; made in Oregon in 1987; machine pieced, machine quilted. $259.00

6171289 – BOTTOM LEFT: LOG CABIN CRIB; 41" x 58"; rose & pink; cotton/polyester; made in Illinois in 1989; machine pieced, hand quilted. $87.00

7171289 – BOTTOM RIGHT: PLAIN QUILT; 109" x 115"; beige; cotton/polyester; made in Illinois in 1989; hand quilted; reversible, back is light blue. $230.00

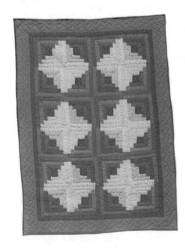

1181289 – TOP LEFT: DAISY; 82" x 94"; blue, green, gold embroidery on white, light blue solid on back; cotton poly blend; made in New York in 1985; hand quilted, cross-stitched. $345.00

2181289 – TOP RIGHT: GEOMETRIC WINDOW; 46" x 61"; blues, greens, rust & peach; cotton & cotton/polyester blends; made in Kansas in 1988; machine pieced, hand quilted; breaks traditional rectangular outlined shaped, has 3-dimensional quality. $288.00

3181289 – CENTER LEFT: VARIETY OF STARS; 88" x 106"; multi-colored; 100% cotton; made in 1989; machine pieced, hand quilted; pre-washed, calico prints in country colors, Mountain Mist batting. $460.00

4181289 – CENTER: ADAPTATION OF LeMOYNE STAR; 36" x 36"; blue &

white; all cotton; made in Maryland in 1989; machine pieced, appliqued & quilted; cotton batting. $87.00

5181289 – CENTER RIGHT: GRAPE MEDALLION; 90" x 114"; navy, gray & burgundy; cottons; made in Missouri in 1984; hand pieced, quilted & appliqued; original design. $1,237.00

6181289 – BOTTOM LEFT: TRIP AROUND THE WORLD – NAVAJO PATTERN; 106" x 108"; terra cotta, brown, cream, monochromatic shades; cottons & blends; made in California in 1985; machine pieced, hand quilted; bonded batting. $748.00

7181289 – BOTTOM RIGHT: OLD MAID'S PUZZLE; 85" x 107"; brights on black; 100% pre-washed cotton; made in Illinois in 1989; machine pieced, hand quilted; Mountain Mist batting. $518.00

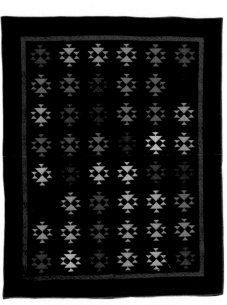

THE American Quilter's Society

invites you to become a member today!

You will receive the quarterly issue of the *American Quilter* magazine plus all of these other benefits for only $15.00 for your one-year membership. Your savings on one AQS book order will probably be more than this low membership fee.

In order to become a member of the American Quilter's Society, send your check or charge card information. You will receive your membership pin and card by return mail.

Membership Pin

Your elegant maroon and gold pin signifies that you have had the vision to join the American Quilter's Society to help promote the art of quilting and set the standard of excellence that all who love quilting desire to achieve.

Quilts for Sale Service

We are offering our members the opportunity to have quilts they would like to sell photographed and listed in a catalog at no expense to members.

National Quilt Show

Free admission for members. Each spring in Paducah, Kentucky, 400 exquisite quilts are displayed with more than $55,000 in cash awards. Workshops, lectures, authors, fashion show and Merchants Mall are also featured.

Savings on Quilting Books

Periodically you will receive a list of many books on quilting. As a member, you can buy any of these books at attractive savings.

American Quilter Magazine

This beautiful, colorful magazine is exclusively for members of AQS. It is not available to the public or on newstands. Spring, Summer, Fall, and Winter issues are sent to you free. You, as a member, can share your experiences, techniques and beautiful creations and promote your accomplishments through this magazine.

Looking to the Future

The society is establishing a National Quilt Museum, Archives and Headquarters with a staff to coordinate activities and help your local clubs in their shows, sales and fund-raising activities. Publication of full-color books to feature quilting and quilters in each state is envisioned. AQS is dedicated to promoting the interests of the quilter.

 American Quilter's Society

P. O. Box 3290 • Paducah, KY 42002-3290

Order Toll-Free
1-800-626-5420
When Using
Visa & MasterCard